LEARNING WITH
READERS THEATRE

LEARNING WITH READERS THEATRE

NEILL DIXON

ANNE DAVIES

COLLEEN POLITANO

PEGUIS PUBLISHERS
WINNIPEG • CANADA

Printed and bound in Canada by Kromar Printing Limited

95 96 97 98 99 5 4 3 2 1

Canadian Cataloguing in Publication Data

Dixon, Neill, 1940–
 Learning with readers theatre
 (Building connections)
 Includes bibliographical references.
 ISBN 1-895411-80-7

1. Readers theater – Study and teaching (Elementary).
2. Reading (Elementary). 3. Language arts (Elementary).
4. Drama in education. I. Davies, Anne, 1955–
II. Politano, Colleen, 1946– III. Title
IV. Series.

 PN2081.R4D5 1996 372.4 C95-920205-6

Editor: Annalee Greenberg
Book and Cover Design: Laura Ayers

Peguis Publishers Limited
100–318 McDermot Avenue
Winnipeg, Manitoba
Canada R3A 0A2
1-800-667-9673

This book is dedicated to the children, parents, and educators
with whom we have had the good fortune to work and learn.
They have taught us many things.

CONTENTS

ACKNOWLEDGMENTS

We'd like to express our appreciation to Dr. William Adams, Director, Institute for Readers Theatre, San Diego, who willingly shared his vast experience and stimulated our thinking and continued growth in the area of Readers Theatre.

Our editor, Annalee Greenberg, continues to try to teach us the intricacies of her craft. Thank you, Annalee, for polishing our rough work. We need your fine editing skills.

With thanks to Caren Cameron and Kathleen Gregory who continue to collaborate with us, especially on the topic of evaluation. We thank them for providing many seeds for the ideas found in the evaluation chapter.

With thanks to Brian Goodwin, Tsolum Elementary School, for permission to use his Readers Theatre scripts for sharing assemblies. Also thanks to Darry Oudendag, Heather Ferraby, and the Tsolum Peacekeepers for allowing us to include the peacekeepers script.

With thanks to Kari Fraser for being such a wonderful teacher and teaching partner.

With thanks to the students and staff of Miracle Beach Elementary School, School District #71 (Courtenay), and Tsolum Elementary School, School District #71 (Courtenay), for building great schools in which to teach, work, and learn.

With thanks to all the students who have taken courses about Readers Theatre with Neill Dixon, and, in particular, to those students who gave permission for their work to be used in this book:

Lorraine Auld	Leah Bradford	Julie Brooker
Alana Check	Sylvia Dakin	Maye Davis
Pat Dodman	Gretchen Dolan	Marta Fiddy
Catherine Galloway	Virgina Garrioch	Gwen Hall
Trish Hawkins	Suzanne Jennings	Julie Johnson
Leona Keltie	Donna Leukov	Cindy Lowry
Pat Lundquist	Jan Maund	Marty Maxwell
Donalda Messer	Cheryl Metcalfe	Liz Moore

Brenda Neufeld   Sharon Niddrie   Ruth Niedziejko

David Osborn   Sue Postans   Jacqueline Poulin

Bridgitte Rathje-Papadakis   Wink Richardson

Rosemary Ronalds   Teri Rychlik   Marion Saunders

Vera Sigmund   Patty Spearman   Pat Sutcliffe

And thanks to our families for continuing to put up with us while giving us their support.

We would like to acknowledge our appreciation to Richard Thompson and Orca Book Publishers for permission to excerpt the section Grandfather's Memories from *Cold Night, Brittle Light* © 1994.

INTRODUCTION

WHO IS THIS BOOK FOR?

Learning With Readers Theatre, a new book in the series Building Connections, is intended for busy elementary teachers who are looking for effective ways to enhance student learning while recognizing the diversity of learners in elementary classrooms. Readers Theatre is one excellent way of doing this. This book can serve as a starting point for teachers who are considering using Readers Theatre for the first time or those wanting to expand their existing repertoire of strategies.

This book includes
- effective ways to plan and organize for Readers Theatre
- successful classroom strategies for making assessment and evaluation an integral part of your learning and teaching
- ideas that practicing classroom teachers have used to integrate learning across disciplines or subject areas
- ideas for organizing Readers Theatre experiences to ensure successful and positive learning and teaching
- ideas for meeting the diverse needs of students
- ideas for building scripts and staging performances
- ideas for connecting Readers Theatre to storytelling
- sample scripts that can be used as is or as jumping-off points for writing your own scripts
- ways of involving students in their own evaluation
- ways to work successfully with others—parents, colleagues, school administrators and community members

Although in this book we share many ideas that have worked in our classrooms, we want to encourage those of you just beginning with Readers Theatre to trust yourself; incorporate only those ideas that will enhance the strategies that already work for you and your students. There are many right ways to teach and learn. We share some of them to make your experiences more positive and to provide support and confirmation for your current successes. This book is an invitation to recognize the expert within each of us.

Articulating Our Beliefs

What is Readers Theatre?

Readers Theatre involves children in oral reading through reading parts in scripts. Unlike traditional theatre, the emphasis is mainly on oral expression of the part. Readers Theatre is "theatre of the imagination."[1] It involves children in understanding their world, creating their own scripts, reading aloud, performing with a purpose, and bringing enjoyment to both themselves and their audiences. Readers Theatre gives children a purpose for writing, for reading, and for sharing their learning by bringing others into the joyful "imagination space"[2] they create. Readers Theatre "succeeds in giving the same suggestive push to the imaginations in the audience that the act of silent reading gives to the imagination of the perceptive silent reader."

1. *Readers Theatre Handbook: A Dramatic Approach to Literature,* by Leslie Irene Coger and Melvin White, published by Scott, Foresman and Company, Glenview, Illinois, 1982 (Third Edition). p.4

2. Ibid. p.5

WHY USE READERS THEATRE?

Readers Theatre provides a real context for reading; self-consciousness or concern about one's reading is lost as readers become involved in the act of creating performance.

Readers Theatre creates a living experience for the audience—it takes written words and makes them multidimensional. Words come alive as the characters interact. Performers bring life and meaning to symbols by vocal and physical means—they work hand in hand with the author of the text to make that which is imaginary real. Students become a real part of the story.

Readers Theatre has obvious benefits for students by increasing their skills as readers, writers, listeners, speakers, and expanding their ability to represent what they know.

As well as expanding children's skill with language arts, **Readers Theatre** animates the concepts taught in mathematics, science, social studies, music, and second-language learning. Children involved in the production of Readers Theatre—scripting, casting, rehearsing, and performing—are learning by doing.

Readers Theatre makes knowledge and information come alive. This shift from passive to active learning creates powerful learning opportunities for students. Research on the brain and on learning clearly confirms the positive impact of active involvement on learning.

Readers Theatre creates confidence, poise, and power as children work together toward shared goals. Children know they are each vital to the success of the work, yet acknowledge the importance of everyone's role—teamwork builds relationships and an appreciation for one another's strengths and differences. Learning with Readers Theatre helps build a strong learning community.

We use **Readers Theatre** because it helps all readers become better readers. Readers Theatre provides troubled readers with successful reading experiences; it can reshape images of failure into those of success and accomplishment. Readers Theatre forms a bridge between troubled reading to supported reading, and ultimately, independent reading.

Readers Theatre

- motivates through engagement
- requires no special equipment
- is easy to use
- is successful for all ability levels
- creates cooperative interactions
- adds liveliness to our classrooms
- supports other teaching methodologies
- joins creativity to learning
- improves self-image through moments of excellence
- teaches oral and written communication along with subject matter
- provides repetition that reinforces comprehension and retention

We use Readers Theatre because it helps us, as teachers, structure successful learning experiences. Readers Theatre helps learners learn more.

WHAT DO WE KNOW ABOUT LEARNERS?

When teachers describe the successes in their classrooms, the same words and phrases come up again and again. When their classroom experiences are successful, they say, their children are

- building on what they already know
- feeling good about themselves and their work
- making some choices
- showing what they know in different ways
- feeling a sense of accomplishment
- working together and by themselves
- knowing that what they say and do is valued by their teachers and their classmates
- finding out that they can learn from others and that others can learn from them
- finding out that they have something to offer others
- seeing teachers as learners
- having fun learning
- excited about sharing what they are doing with others
- talking about what they are doing and how they are doing it

Current research that describes how children learn parallels teachers' descriptions of successful learning experiences. Combining what teachers are saying about their successes and what the researchers are reporting about their findings, the evidence is clear. Effective learning takes place when students

- want to learn and need to learn
- realize what they have learned
- enjoy what they are doing
- can relate what they are doing to their total experience
- are able to take risks
- feel a sense of support
- talk about their new knowledge with others
- feel good about themselves
- have opportunities to work with others
- make some decisions
- have a chance to touch, smell, see, hear, feel, think

What do you believe about learning and learners?

These same characteristics apply whether talking about children learning to read or write, learning about math, science, or their world. Learning is not dependent upon age or what is being learned. Learners are learners are learners.

All teachers have beliefs about learners. When teachers can articulate these beliefs clearly, they are able to screen every element of their practice by asking whether or not these are in alignment with their beliefs.

DOES USING READERS THEATRE MAKE SENSE?

The main purpose of Readers Theatre is to promote learning. Readers Theatre provides many opportunities for learning that is relevant, connected, fun, purposeful, allows choice, and makes connections with the world in which our students live. Readers Theatre works best for us when we consider the total needs of our children and use the differences among them to explore the similarities and to invite new learning.

Relevance is important because all people learn when it has meaning for them.

Learning has meaning for children when it is relevant. Learning becomes relevant when it is based on children's interests, needs, and abilities. Learning increases in relevance when children are given the opportunity to represent their knowledge in a variety of ways.

Connections are important, because learning is more lasting and significant when we can integrate what we are learning with what we already know.

Identifying and inviting connections between kids and topics, between kids and kids, between classes and classes, between school and the community, between old knowledge and new knowledge, and between process and content increases the opportunity for learning. The experience of constructing knowledge together gives learners opportunities not only to connect with each other but to connect their own knowledge in ways that are lasting and meaningful for them.

Fun is essential. When learning is joyful people think of it with pleasure and want to learn more and more.

Feeling a sense of accomplishment, realizing that you discovered something you didn't know before, and finding out that you can learn from others and that others can learn from you—that is fun. Having a shared purpose and learning from each other is joyful. Readers Theatre stimulates shared conversations that lead to more learning. With Readers Theatre, children use expression to convey meaning in a variety of ways and are members of effective, broad-based learning communities.

Choice allows for ownership because it respects the uniqueness of each individual.

Having a choice is a powerful motivator for learners. Teachers can provide a common focus to learners of different ages and different interests while allowing each student to build upon his or her own strengths, interests, and experiences. Side-by-side learning increases both *what* can be learned and *how* it can be learned. With Readers Theatre we build on and plan for diversity.

We learn when we know there is a real purpose to what we are doing.

When using Readers Theatre, teachers and students work together to increase the purposefulness of learning. We increase the connections to real audiences for our reading, writing, and performing, and design real ways to help in our school and our community. Our students have differing talents, skills, and ideas. Readers Theatre encourages learners to make their learning more meaningful while representing it in a different way.

Integration of subject areas and interests is natural. Readers Theatre offers us a way to erase the lines that schools have created within and among the traditional disciplines and typical school timetables.

Learning is easier when we see what form it might take and how it might be accomplished. Our ability to learn is enhanced when we see the larger context for what is being learned. When we use Readers Theatre, we encourage children to make connections between subject areas and recognize that language is an integral part of all learning and knowing.

GETTING STARTED WITH READERS THEATRE

INTRODUCING READERS THEATRE

For three readers

All:	Readers Theatre...Readers Theatre...Readers Theatre...
Reader 1:	Readers Theatre.
Reader 2:	What is it?
Reader 1:	It is reading.
Reader 3:	Reading a script...
Reader 2:	as a character...
Reader 1:	as a storyteller.
Reader 3:	It is theatre...
Reader 2:	that isn't memorized...
Reader 1:	and we can read more than one part...
Reader 2:	by changing our voices.
Reader 1:	Readers Theatre is...
Reader 3:	an audience listening...
Reader 2:	using imagination...
Reader 3:	to picture the scenes.
Reader 1:	It is theatre...
Reader 2:	about people,
Reader 3:	ordinary people,
Reader 2:	whose lives are exciting...
Reader 1:	sad...
Reader 3:	humdrum...
Reader 2:	and strange.
Reader 1:	Readers Theatre is entertaining.
Reader 3:	It is acting with the voice...
Reader 2:	without scenery...
Reader 3:	makeup or props.
Reader 1:	Readers Theatre is challenging.
Reader 3:	Readers Theatre is the voice of the people.
Reader 2:	It is sharing literature.
All:	Readers Theatre!

What do you already know about Readers Theatre?

What would you like to learn more about?

The above script outlines the basics of Readers Theatre; it is the presentation of literature by two or more readers who interpret the mood of the text. The readers may take the parts of the narrators or characters and employ those techniques of expression which bring the text alive for an audience. Readers Theatre is

Readers
- using scripts
- reading the story

Audience
- hearing and seeing the story
- imagining

Props
- none are required but they may be used with restraint to enhance the script

Roles

Director
- motivates the readers and assists them to both interpret and communicate the meaning of the script
- assists with the "blocking" of the readers (i.e. placement of the readers on the stage in relationship to one another and the audience)

Narrator
- weaves the story around the characters to show their relationships
- sometimes focuses on the audience and other times focuses on the characters. This is referred to as an *offstage focus* (audience) or an *onstage focus* (characters).

Characters
- bring action to the story in the minds of the audience. They can have both an onstage and offstage focus depending on which best delivers the mood of the story.

GETTING STARTED WITH STUDENTS

Following is the basic process for preparing and performing Readers Theatre:

1. Choose a script or scripts (select a prepared script, adapt a literary selection, or write a new script—see chapters 5 and 7).

2. Work with students to establish roles (director, narrator, or character).

3. Read, read, read.

4. Practice, practice, practice (see chapters 3 and 4).

5. Perform (see chapters 6 and 9).

PLANNING FOR READERS THEATRE

When we decide to use Readers Theatre to structure the learning in our classroom, we ask ourselves a set of questions that helps us determine the value of Readers Theatre for our students:

- What is there about using Readers Theatre that makes it relevant to my students?
- What opportunities for making connections does Readers Theatre offer? Between children and their world? Between what they know, want to know, and need to know? Between and among themselves?
- What makes me think that Readers Theatre would be enjoyable for my students?
- How does Readers Theatre provide student choice and a range of interests, strengths, and abilities?
- Why is Readers Theatre a good use of my time and my students' time? Will valuable learning come out of this?
- Does using Readers Theatre give my students an opportunity to use a variety of learning processes?
- What curriculum content and processes could Readers Theatre address?

Why would you choose to use Readers Theatre with your students?

And the last and most important question is:

- Do my students feel secure, respected, cared for, appreciated, and supported in their learning?

As elementary teachers, we make decisions about the way we organize the learning in our classrooms. Our purpose in using Readers Theatre is to enhance learning. These questions inform and guide our teaching practice based on what we believe about learners. By using these questions, we increase our chances of using Readers Theatre to provide more opportunities for children to construct new knowledge and increase their repertoire of skills and processes.

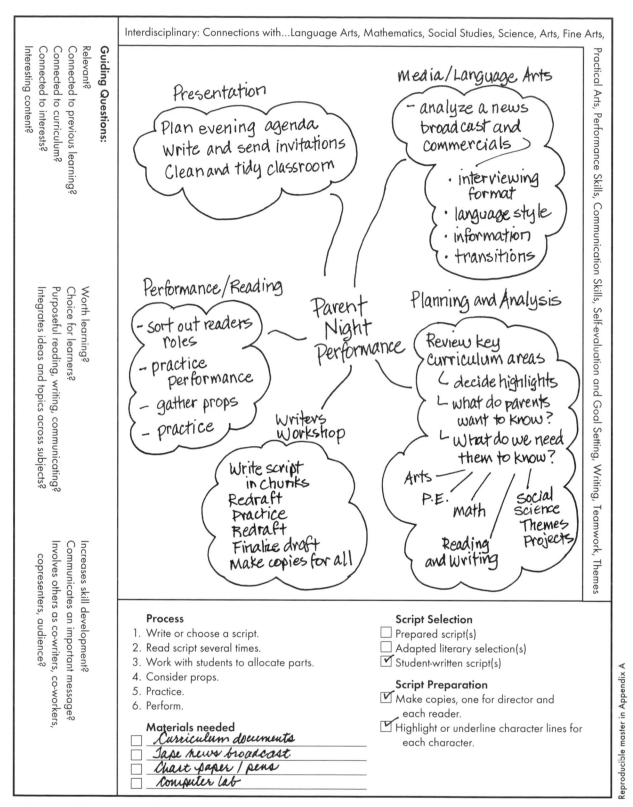

Guiding Questions:

Relevant?
Connected to previous learning?
Connected to curriculum?
Connected to interests?
Interesting content?

Worth learning?
Choice for learners?
Purposeful reading, writing, communicating?
Integrates ideas and topics across subjects?

Increases skill development?
Communicates an important message?
Involves others as co-writers, co-workers, copresenters, audience?

Presentation

Plan evening agenda
Write and send invitations
Clean and tidy classroom

Media/Language Arts

- analyze a news broadcast and commercials
- interviewing format
- language style
- information
- transitions

Performance/Reading

- sort out readers roles
- practice performance
- gather props
- practice

Parent Night Performance

Planning and Analysis

Review key curriculum areas
  ∟ decide highlights
  ∟ what do parents want to know?
  ∟ what do we need them to know?

Arts
P.E.
math
Reading and Writing
Social Science Themes Projects

Writers Workshop

Write script in chunks
Redraft
Practice
Redraft
Finalize draft
Make copies for all

Process
1. Write or choose a script.
2. Read script several times.
3. Work with students to allocate parts.
4. Consider props.
5. Practice.
6. Perform.

Materials needed
☐ Curriculum documents
☐ Tape news broadcast
☐ Chart paper / pens
☐ Computer lab

Script Selection
☐ Prepared script(s)
☐ Adapted literary selection(s)
☑ Student-written script(s)

Script Preparation
☑ Make copies, one for director and each reader.
☑ Highlight or underline character lines for each character.

Reproducible master in Appendix A

Planning sheet for Readers Theatre

ORAL INTERPRETATION

Oral interpretation lies at the heart of Readers Theatre. The reader uses vocal expression to give the listener a vivid picture of the action.

There are many ways to say a sentence. There is a noticeable difference between saying "Come here" in an angry and annoyed voice than saying it in a secretive whisper. That is oral interpretation at its simplest.

In the classroom there are a number of exercises for helping children become aware of their expression and then improving upon it. This chapter outlines several of these strategies or ideas.

What kinds of language strengths do your students already have to bring to Readers Theatre?

🧩 *Oral Interpretation:* ONE SENTENCE

It is important that children notice that different contexts can transform a sentence. In Readers Theatre, narrators and character readers need to experiment to see the many meanings that can be extracted from one sentence.

1. Take one sentence, such as "Mom wants to see you," and emphasize a different word each time.

   Mom (*not Dad or Susie*) wants to see you!

   Mom **wants** (*longing*) to see you.

   Mom wants to **see** (*So there! You're in trouble now*) you.

   Mom wants to see **you**. (*She didn't want to see me after all.*)

2. Have students write short sentences and emphasize a different word with each reading.

3. Have students perform their variations for the class.

🧩 *Oral Interpretation:* VOCAL COLORING

These are the words, often single adverbs, that you sometimes find italicized in parentheses in a script alongside the character's name. For example:

   Ian (*angrily*): I told him I'm not going!"

   Julie (*keeping the secret*): "Our stories have to be the same."

These clues help the director and actor set the correct context and emotions for the action. The following exercise is good for understanding characters and their motivation. It also encourages students to discuss the context—the events both before and after the words they are saying.

1. Have students group themselves in twos or threes and send them off to their own space. Give each group sentences such as the following to read (on a one-page handout or on sentence strips—you'll find a full selection in Appendix A.).

(**Surprised**) Well, hi! I didn't know you were coming tobogganing!

- -

(**Wistfully**) I wish she'd let me have one more piece of birthday cake.

- -

(**Bellowing**) Get out of there...and don't come back, do you hear me?

- -

(**Angrily**) I told you to go to your room. Now will you do as you're told?

- -

(**Frightened**) Who is it? Who's there? Don't come near me...Don't! Don't!

- -

2. Have students take turns saying the sentences to each other, making sure they understand the descriptive clues and are able to show the appropriate emotion in their voices (we suggest you limit the number for younger students). Have students keep track of the emotions they are able to add to their voices, with a view to constantly expanding their repertoire.

Vocal-coloring sentences

3. After students have practiced the various emotions, take the vocal-coloring clues and switch them from sentence to sentence. Consider having students develop their own repertoire of vocal coloring.

Extension: Have students select sentences from favorite stories and provide information about the characters' motivation or emotion. These samples can then be provided to different groups of students for practicing.

✖ *Oral Interpretation:* POLYPHONIC PROSE

Polyphonic prose features devices such as alliteration or onomatopoeia that color the piece with sound; for example, "slithery, sliding, snakes slipping sideways," or "The wind moves around the cement structures of the concrete town, rising and following the walls of the building." When readers portray the sound referred to by a word, they help the audience create the meaning.

Encourage students to look for sounds in words. A knowledge of onomatopoeia will help here. For example, such phrases as, "the lowing cattle," "the bleating sheep," "the swish of the tall grasses," could describe a country scene. Highlighted onomatopoeic words encourage children to create the picture with their voices.

Try the following:

1. Tell students about words that have sounds, using examples such as *hissing, sliding, squelching,* and *splashing.*

2. Students practice saying the sound words and collect more words. Make a list of words and post in classroom. Put sounds in categories, for example, animal sounds, weather sounds, water sounds, and vehicle sounds.

3. Once enough words have been collected, students create sentences that carry the same sound throughout, for example: "The waves splashed on the seashore," or "The wind whistled through the window."

✖ *Oral Interpretation:* ORAL READING

Many children read well, with good expression, from an early age. They naturally incorporate many of the elements of oral interpretation in all their oral reading. Everyone's reading, no matter how good, can be improved through teaching.

To read well, children need to understand the selection, the characters, and the emotion of the piece—knowing why a character says something helps readers match the emotion with their voice. With very young children, using a book such as *Going on a Lion Hunt* (Rosen & Oxenbury 1989) encourages them to get caught up in the excitement of the hunt and use appropriate voice and hand movements. Older children appreciate books such as *The Bedspread*, by Sylvia Fair (1982).

In this book, two sisters are fed up, bored with their living situation:

> "I'm fed up," complained Maude.
> "You're not half as fed up as I am," sulked Amelia.
> "Oh yes I am, " insisted Maude.

Early in the story we find that Maude is the formal "my-way-is-the-right-way" sister and Amelia is more creative and relaxed. The style in which readers interpret each character reflects these traits.

The reading of this story is aided by the descriptive clues that the author includes continually. For example, the author has Amelia and Maude speaking sharply, sulkily, excitedly, and severely. Even when these more obvious clues are not available, there are other contextual clues showing how a character responds to a comment. Mood, setting, and emotions are all considered.

While *The Bedspread* is an excellent book for practice, any book with expressive characters can be used. Following is the process for practicing oral reading:

1. Teacher reads the entire story aloud to the class, using expression.

2. Each student reads to feel the moods and emotions of the characters and to practice their own expressive "mumble" reading—reading that is neither silent nor loud enough for others to hear.

3. Discuss the different motivation of the characters with the students. Ask students to suggest ways of altering vocal coloring through pacing and emotion.

4. Provide practice time for students, with classmates acting as audience for the different interpretations. Have children record notes on the script to remind themselves of the way they want to read the script.

5. Have students present their renditions to their classmates.

6. Have groups of students select other favorite stories and prepare their reading for the class.

✿ *Oral Interpretation:* CLUE, CONTEXT, SENTENCE

Encouraging students to experiment with a wide range of vocal coloring builds a solid foundation for reading any story or script aloud. The following activity challenges them to expand their skills. To do it, you will need three sets of colored cards.

1. On the first set of cards print descriptive speech clues, such as *excitedly, sadly, bravely,* and *agreeably.*

2. Print a selections of sentences such as, "I didn't mean it," and "Don't come near me" on a second color of card.

3. On the third set of colored cards print a collection of possible settings or contexts, such as "three people keeping a secret," "during a fire drill", or "on the jungle gym."

4. Have students group themselves in threes. Have each group select a card from each of the three categories and then rehearse their sentence, using their descriptive speech clue and keeping the selected setting in mind.

5. Each group then reads the sentence, using the descriptive clues (vocal coloring). Classmates try to guess which descriptive clue and context is being used. (When students are first being introduced to this vocabulary, consider having them draw faces displaying the appropriate emotion beside the word to remind them of its meaning.)

6. After this has been introduced and used as a whole-class activity, consider setting up an activity center in the class where students can continue their language play.

Descriptive clues

willingly	bravely	excitedly
angrily	protesting innocence	stubborn
firmly	reminding	bitterly
guiltily	sadly	suddenly
in pain	warning of danger	happily
decisively	agreeably	enthusiastically
selfishly	severely	argumentatively
complaining	persistently	exclaiming loudly
sharply in anger	breathless with excitement	
remembering past events		

Sentences

- ☛ I didn't mean it.
- ☛ Don't come near me.
- ☛ I'd really like to play with her/him.
- ☛ How long will you be?

- Shut the door.
- You'll never catch me.
- Don't let them hear you.
- Go to your room.

Contexts/Situation
- three people keeping a secret
- child explaining to a parent
- parent explaining to a very young child
- parent explaining to an angry child
- child daring another child to do something
- police officer speaking to another adult in a hospital emergency ward
- teacher speaking to a rowdy class
- teacher speaking to a group of children working
- three good friends playing together

Oral Interpretation: SUBTEXT

Subtext is the meaning implied by an utterance. For example, take a short sentence, "It is time," and look for many possible meanings for it. Say the line to indicate the following meanings:

> You said you'd have my order ready by now.
> I told you when.
> You must be ready by now.
> I don't want to hurry you but...
> Isn't the bus usually here by now?

What other subtexts can you devise?

Subtext exercise

Devise a number of subtexts for each of the following lines

Is this yours?

I love chocolate.

When are you going?

I've already been there.

Mary is here.

The book is by June Lyons.

I wish I could go.

Names: John, Iran, Sayla, Nicole, Ben.

Date : _____

Is this yours?

1.) I think it's mine.

2.) Do you really want it?

3.) Is it somebody else's?

4.) Who does this belong to, anyways!

5.) Who didn't clean up this mess up?

✲ *Oral Interpretation:* TONGUE TWISTERS

The tongue twisters here are used to practice enunciation. The idea is to sound the consonants clearly so that each word is clear on its own; words should not run into each other.

1. Teacher distributes tongue twisters the students are able to read, either written on cards or as a handout, and reads them.

2. Students take turns saying a tongue twister slowly and with clarity, emphasizing the consonants, practicing with classmates:

The wil**d** win**d** whippe**d** wha**t** fro**m** the whar**f**.

Not:

Thewilewinwhipptwhafrothewharf.

Encourage students to play with the tongue twisters, going faster and slower and noting the effect of speed.

> **What other kinds of language play do you know that would encourage students to stretch their skills?**

Tongue twisters

The wild wind whipped what from the wharf.

This thistle seems like that thistle.

A black-backed bath brush

The seething sea ceaseth seething.

Tom threw Tim three thumbtacks.

Old oily Ollie oils oily Oldsmobiles.

The big black bug bit the big black bear and made the big black bear bleed blood.

The skunk sat on a stump and thunk the stump stunk, but the stump thunk the skunk stunk.

A pale pink proud peacock pompously preened its pretty plumage.

Reproducible master in Appendix A

4

STORYTELLING

Storytelling is a natural form of communication, appropriate for everyone. When we listened to our parents tell us about their lives, we formed pictures using our imaginations. Often these stories touched our hearts and provided us with insights into our heritage. Through hearing stories, children are motivated to read, develop a love of language, and improve their listening skills, vocabulary, comprehension, sequencing, and recall. Listening to stories also connects children to their own culture and the culture of others.

The storytelling experience has lots to teach children. If students apply the elements of oral interpretation to their reading and storytelling, they gain confidence in themselves, have a good understanding of character development, and are able to hold the attention of an audience.

Effective storytellers tell stories they like and think their audience will like, and limit the number of characters. Simple stories can be elaborated on as the storyteller becomes more familiar and comfortable with the text and the role of storyteller.

The storyteller holds the pictures in her imagination so that she is retelling what she sees, not words that have been memorized. Trying to recall the whole story word by word rather than interpreting pictures from the imagination gets in the way of effective storytelling. The storyteller interprets a story for the audience by varying tone, expressions, and inflections. This vocal coloring allows the audience to understand the story as the teller intends it.

Storytelling brings literature alive by creating patterns and images in the minds of the listeners. Storytelling is a means of entertainment, an educational aid, a therapeutic device. In Readers Theatre, each reader is a storyteller, interpreting mood, action, intent, and plot through his or her character. Storytelling is limited to one, or sometimes two, people conveying the message. Readers Theatre and storytelling are alike in spirit and form.

We all have stories. We want to retell these stories to hold the attention of an audience. This chapter provides suggestions and outlines for helping our students increase their storytelling confidence and ability.

Storytelling:

🧩 *Storytelling:* STORYTELLING PRACTICE IDEAS

Children grow up knowing many stories—family tales, fables, folk tales, fairy tales, myths and legends. Some of these stories come from books. Others are told orally. Some of these stories are traditional tales; others are unique to the homeland or the culture of an individual's family.

When preparing stories, it is important to limit the number of characters and description and include lots of action. The story-teller must remember each character's motivation and the tone for each voice to ensure the parts are not confused. Some younger children may limit the subjects of their stories to their mom, dad, or siblings. Others may include other well-known people whom they are able to mimic.

When students hear these stories and, in turn, share them as family cultural treasures, they are able to connect with their peers through their heritage. Students who learn to tell familiar stories to an audience learn to portray mood through words and expression, skills that can then be used in Readers Theatre.

Following are two ideas for practicing storytelling:

1. Have students interview their parents for more details about their family history or about favorite stories they were told when they were young (consider using the book *When I Was Young In the Mountain* by Cynthia Rylant to prompt parents' memories).

2. Students then draw or record their story sequence in five to seven parts.

3. Each child practices telling his or her story.

4. Each child tells the story to others.

Another idea is to have children challenge their imagination and tell an impromptu story about an object.

1. Fill a bag with many different and unusual things such as tongs, shears, keys, a candleholder, hat, bodkin, garlic press, egg slicer, sponge, fountain pen, stuffed animal, and so on.

2. Have groups of three or four students take an object from the bag.

3. Have the groups create a story around the object they have chosen. Give the groups enough time to do this. All group members should have a part in telling the story to the class.

✹ *Storytelling:* BODY LANGUAGE

Nonverbal language communicates attitudes between individuals. The ways a person sits, folds arms, or stands can imply a variety of feelings. In Readers Theatre, body language allows a reader to feel a character as well as communicate that character more fully to the audience.

Try the following exercise for practicing body language:

1. Explain the concept of body language to students.

2. Ask different students to communicate a message or demonstrate an emotion, such as bravery, anger, excitement, or guilt, using body language.

3. Have partners or small groups of students portray a sentence from the following list:

   - Oh, how boring.
   - I'm freezing.
   - Please enter.
   - I'm not sure what you mean.
   - Look out!
   - You've got to be joking!
   - I'm really concerned about you.
   - Keep away!
   - I would like to help.
   - Please help me.

   Talk about what is effective and why it is effective.

4. Generate a list of common body-language signals with students and record on chart paper.

5. Have students work in groups to generate more sentences for class members to act out.

✿ *Storytelling:* EXPRESSION OF TONE

Learning to convey a character's message through tone of voice is essential for effective Readers Theatre, storytelling, and reading aloud. This activity, similar to vocal coloring in the previous chapter, helps students isolate different moods and change the meaning of sentences by varying voice tone. It involves creating a list of voice tones that can determine the underlying meaning of a sentence.

1. Prepare cards by printing on them different words describing tone, such as *sad, rude, frustrated, lazy, happy, nervous, angry, amused, bullying, furious, disinterested, suspicious.*

2. Write a sentence (for example, "I'm sick and I can't go to school," or "What are you doing?") where all students are able to see it.

3. Read it in a monotone voice and then ask everyone to read it with you. Talk about how the reader feels when reading in a monotone (words such as *bored, disinterested,* or *uncaring* may be used).

4. Display one of the tone words. Talk about the associated emotion and ask students to put the tone and the sentence together—to read the sentence in such a way that the emotion is infused in each word.

5. Have students suggest other emotionally laden words and make a list. Cards can be made of these words and added to the existing collection.

6. Once students are comfortable with this activity, ask them to break into smaller groups and practice varying the tone of different sentences.

Put these cards in an activity center to encourage even more language play.

✹ *Storytelling:* VOICE TEMPO

Conveying expression with one's voice depends upon the readers' ability to vary the speed or *tempo* of the words. In the following activity students practice varying the tempo and see the impact on the meaning:

1. Develop a list of sentences with students that can be used to practice tempo. Some examples are

    -   The snow is falling and school has been canceled.
    -   A big, big dog tried to play with me.
    -   The car is coming around the corner.
    -   The principal is away today.
    -   We had a substitute teacher today.
    -   They discovered a new set of dinosaur bones last week at the river.
    -   There was a student lost during the ski trip.

2. Ask students to repeat the sentences in the following different ways to experience the impact of tempo on meaning:

    -   quickly, to show excitement
    -   slowly, to indicate disappointment
    -   moderately, to state a fact (like on radio or television news reports)

3. Practice the sentences together as a class, in small groups, and independently during activity time.

✹ *Storytelling:* CHARACTER PROBLEM-SOLVING

When readers know what the problem is, they are able to understand the motivation behind a character's actions. Then the mood of the character becomes clearer and can be more easily portrayed by the reader. Students have to understand different motives and how they might impact on a character's mood. The following activity provides practice time for students with common characters, common situations, and common problems:

1. Prepare a collection of cards, each with a character, a setting, or a problem. Color code each kind of card (for example, character cards with a blue stripe, setting cards with a red stripe, and problem cards with a green stripe) or have a different color card for each type. You can also photocopy the cards supplied in Appendix A.

2. Talk with students about the different kinds of characters, settings, and problems found in stories.

3. Select one card from each collection and, as a class, brainstorm all the possible stories. Repeat until students seem comfortable with the task.

4. Have students form small groups, select different cards, and create a story. For a quick, fun brainstormed story, give students a limited amount of time. This activity is intended to be impromptu!

5. Have groups of students present their stories. (Warning: This activity should be full of fun, enthusiasm, and laughter. If not, proceed with caution.)

Character, setting, and problem cards

butcher	lawyer	carpenter
painter	writer	farmer
fisher	police officer	flight attendant
hair stylist	pilot	actor
teenager	gardener	horse rider
soccer field	mall	country farm
hotel	classroom	house
boat cruise	ship	theater
broken water pipes	angry dog	hole in the boat
flat tire	head wind	empty box

🧩 *Storytelling:* STORIES FROM AN INANIMATE OBJECT'S PERSPECTIVE

Portraying a variety of characters allows students to see life from other perspectives. In this activity students pretend they are inanimate objects telling about some of the events in their life. They describe how others deal with them.

This activity builds confidence because there is no wrong or right answer; the possibilities are unlimited. When students practice seeing, feeling, and then speaking as that character, they develop vital Readers Theatre skills.

1. Have students create a list of inanimate objects.

2. Ask each student to select one (you might choose to have them working in pairs or small groups to stimulate discussion and ideas) and *become* that object, describing life from their perspective.

3. Ask students to share their ideas either verbally or in writing. Consider dividing the class into groups of five to seven to take turns presenting their work.

Hacky Jack

I'm a hacky sack and I'm purple, blue, and yellow. People hit me up and see how many times they can hit me up. Or, they can rally which means three or more people are in a circle and everyone hits to see how many they can get. Sometimes I get wet so all my insides grow and make me hard. When people first hit me it hurt but I adapted to it so now I don't notice it as much. It's not fun being a hack because all people do is hit you and you get bruised. I like it when people play with me on grass because when they miss I'll hit the soft grass.

Student writing samples: inanimate objects

- Oh, no, it's coming, it's coming!
- Auggh, it's got me.
- Those dirty fingers all sweaty and slimy.
- Ohhh, not the cold water.
- Why cold?
- Haven't those inferior life-forms heard of warm water?
- How uncivilized.
- The water.
- Those hands scrubbing so vigorously. I can feel my skull eroding away. The pain. The fall — the hands just slip away with not but a second thought. I drop into a hard cold bed. Can you believe they never rinse me off?
- And just think, in their ingenious ways, they've invented liquid soap. It pains me to think of all those innocent bars of soap creamed in the most painful of ways. Just so they can wash their hands a little faster.
- Alas, what am I but a bar of soap.

✽ Storytelling: REMEMBERING A SPECIAL PLACE

Storytelling involves building narrative around anecdotes. Telling anecdotes well involves practice—students must focus on the important events, tell them in sequence, and add expression/mood. This not only improves their conversation skills but also prepares them for Readers Theatre. Try the following activity to develop these skills:

1. Ask students to recall a detailed picture of a memorable/special place. Explain that it could be a hiding place, a place where something wonderful (or awful) happened, a holiday spot, a garden, or the inside of your home. It must be a real place.

2. Everyone takes a few minutes and sketches, with words or lines, as many details of their place as possible.

3. Pair students off. Ask half the students to tell their partner as many things as they can remember about their place. When finished, the partners retell as much of the description as possible and asks, "Is there anything else?" This is repeated until as many details as possible are recalled and retold.

4. Ask the other half of the class to tell their partners as many things as they can remember about their memorable place, using their sketch to assist their description. When finished, the partner retells as much of the description as possible and asks, "Is there anything else?" This is repeated until as many details as possible are recalled and retold.

5. Students can continue to add details to the word or line sketch until the special place is fully described. The activity could end at this point, or teachers could ask students to write a detailed description of the special place.

Student writing samples: Remembering a Special Place

In a elevator

One day I was going to canucks game. When we where on the ferry me and my friend Tyler went on the elevator down to my car to get a drink. We were going down and I pressed all the bottons and the elevator stopped. I said oh no were stuck so I pressed the alarm botton about fifty times and some people got us out. I told my dad that I got stuck on the elevator and it was scary then he said I know because I heard the alarm go off. Then the ferry dock and we were on our way.

A year ago my step dad had a heart transplant I remember my uncle came to my school and picked me up. When we were in his car he told me that Jim was paged to go to the hospital. A few minutes after we got home they came and took my step dad to the Vancouver hospital. All my relatives were crying. I told them all to stop crying because Jim will be ok. My uncle Don would not stop crying because he was the closest one out of all my relatives. The night before this happened we were joking about Jim having to go to the hospital befor his wedding. Jim was told by his doctors they don't know what caused the disease in his heart. The heart came from an 18 year old girl. She died in a car accident. We named my little sisters middle name after her.

✳ *Storytelling:* READING ALOUD TO CHILDREN

Adults read aloud to model character development, to expose children to quality literature, to extend their reading range, to improve their listening skills, to provide a stimulus for their imagination, and for sheer enjoyment!

Teachers know from both experience and research that children's ability to understand complex language is greater when children listen to stories than when they read to themselves. Listening to stories builds children's knowledge base and supports their reading growth.

Text is brought to life when the feelings, thoughts, and actions of the characters are made as real as possible. As it is when telling stories or narrating stories from a Readers Theatre script, the task of the story reader is to bring the text to life. When children listen to stories read aloud, they learn some of the skills of effective reading and storytelling. These experiences help children when they read, tell stories, or perform Readers Theatre.

Reading aloud to children requires

- ☛ choosing a story to read
- ☛ preparing to read the story
- ☛ reading the story

Choose quality literature for reading aloud. The many anthologies of short stories, poetry, and selected chapters from novels are a good source. Anthologies often include suggestions for listening ages and the length of time a story takes to read. Your classroom

and school library can be the source of many wonderful stories to read aloud. Jim Trelease's books are full of excellent recommendations for such books (See Bibliography, page 153, for complete bibliographic information.).

Stories are brought to life when the reader visualizes the events and then, through expressive reading, enables the listeners to form their own images of the story. This happens when the reader has time to prepare by reading the story in advance. Preparation is important for understanding the sequence of events in the story and the building blocks of the climax, or resolution, of the story.

The physical act of reading to a group is also important. Seated comfortably on a stool or chair, preferably slightly above the audience, the reader has a view of the listeners. Frequent eye contact allows the performer to "read" the listeners. Turning pages without disrupting the flow of the story provides a better reading experience for the audience. Some people hold the book in both hands, others rest it on their knees or on a music stand, while others hold it with one hand.

Readers can enhance the story reading by gesturing to provide clarity in a story. Where a character makes a fist or waves goodbye, for example, the reader can mime the actions. A definite "No!" can be indicated by a shake of the head. There are moments in all stories when a gesture adds another dimension to the interpretation.

Accents and dialects may also be used to enhance readings. A light touch is recommended, these should not overdone as they can interfere with the clarity of the reading. An occasional gesture or smattering of an accent is sufficient; too much will have the audience listening to the accent rather than the story.

Watching stories read aloud helps children become more fluent readers. Smooth and fluid reading is modeled through expression, enunciation, pitch, tone, and volume. As children become familiar with these attributes, they gain experience and skill in their own readings. Everybody loves having stories read well to them—no matter how old they are!

Is it time to revisit your favorite children's stories to see if they'd make wonderful stories to tell or to use for writing scripts?

WRITING SCRIPTS

5

A good variety of scripts is essential to maintain interest while students learn techniques, strategies, and processes related to Readers Theatre. Some scripts are developed through brainstorming about a theme, conversations between a protagonist and an antagonist, or discussions among friends. Short stories written during writers workshop and popular published stories can be turned into scripts for your own classroom.

Three key sources for Readers Theatre scripts are prepared scripts, adapted literary selections, and student-written scripts. The choice you make depends upon your purpose as well as your students' interests and abilities. If you select a prepared script, there are many resources available to you (see Bibliography, page 153, for some recommendations).

Students can write and perform their own scripts. There are three structures for writing simple Readers Theatre scripts:

- a list of descriptive words and phrases
- a collection of relevant categories within a main topic, with descriptive words clustered within each category
- words ordered to create increasing impact

Following is the process for writing a Readers Theatre script:

1. Create a giant brainstormed list or web of everything about the topic selected.
2. Categorize ideas from the list or web into major groups.
3. Divide into parts for readers.
4. Draft and revise the script.
5. Consider aids (costumes, music, lighting, props) that could improve the script.
6. Practice the final draft.
7. Present.

The process for adapting a selection is slightly different:

1. Select a part of a story or written work that meets your needs.
2. Underline the names of the characters.

3. List the cast and add needed narration.

4. Draft and revise the script.

5. Underline or highlight each character's lines.

6. Consider aids (costumes, music, lighting, props) that could improve the script.

7. Practice the final draft.

8. Present the Readers Theatre.

In this chapter we discuss in more detail how to write scripts based on personal experience, familiar stories, conversations, and published literature.

Writing Scripts:

Writing Scripts: THEME SCRIPTS

These are simple scripts developed by brainstorming all the ideas students have on a topic. They are often limited to one word per line.

For example, one group of grade two and three students had been studying forests, focusing on the use of timber, related ecology, and conservation. During the study, they took field trips to the bush, around the school, and to a sawmill. They examined fallen trees and strips left from logging. From these experiences they developed the ideas, wrote the script, and practiced and performed their enthusiastic production, a process that took less than one hour. Depending on your students' experience working with Readers Theatre and with one another, decide whether students are going to write a script together or divide into smaller groups and write more than one script.

Try the following process to create theme scripts:

1. Have students list all the things they have learned.

2. Help students group similar ideas, words, and concepts to create larger categories. In the example described above, children decided on the categories *beauty, fun, magic,* and *usefulness.*

3. List all the words and phrases for each category.

4. Group students in groups of five. Give various lines to individual readers within each group and have them practice.

5. Rehearse by reading the entire script together so everyone is familiar with the script. Then have individual readers read their own lines.

Student-created script about forests

Forests

All readers:	Forests.		**All readers:**	Forests are fun...
Reader 1:	What are they?		**Reader 5:**	...Climb a tree.
Reader 2:	Groups of trees that...		**Reader 4:**	Swing off branches.
Reader 3:	...give off oxygen,		**Reader 1:**	Build a fort.
Reader 4:	grow to different sizes,		**Reader 2:**	Pick mushrooms.
Reader 5:	give glue from sap,		**Reader 3:**	Jump in the leaves.
Reader 1:	provide paper		**Reader 5:**	Explore.
Reader 2:	and shade,		**Reader 1:**	Walk across logs
Reader 4:	are animals' homes,		**Reader 2:**	and eat berries.
Reader 5:	produce lumber			
Reader 3:	and firewood.		**All readers:**	Forests are magic...
			Reader 4:	...things appear,
All readers:	Forests are beautiful...		**Reader 1:**	then disappear.
Reader 1:	...all sorts of colors,		**Reader 5:**	Winds and sounds,
Reader 3:	many plants,		**Reader 3:**	storms and light,
Reader 4:	wild animals,		**Reader 2:**	shade and shadows,
Reader 2:	colorful berries,		**Reader 5:**	camouflage,
Reader 3:	different sounds,		**Reader 4:**	fire!
Reader 1:	burbling creeks.		**All readers:**	Forests!

Once the students are comfortable with their lines, consider visiting other classes to perform.

✱ *Writing Scripts:* CELEBRATING A HOLIDAY

Celebrate a holiday by having children share their views and past experiences, then collaborating to create a shared script. In this way every child's experiences are accepted and valued by classmates. When writing Readers Theatre from one's own experiences, every child is "correct."

Try the following process for creating a holiday script:

1. Select a holiday.

2. Decide what you want students to learn.

3. Decide on how to write the script: as a class script, in small groups, or in pairs.

4. As a group, brainstorm associations, words, and events that students connect with the celebration. If needed, help students group together similar ideas, words, and concepts. Record all contributions and leave on display.

5. Provide time for students to talk, write, and prepare their presentation. Print copies of the script in large primary style text for easy reading. An extension of this activity entails having students electing and placing mood words that help convey meaning to the audience.

6. Present.

Christmas Is More Than Presents

by Division 13

Narrator 1: Christmas is more than presents. Christmas is...
Reader 1: Sharing, caring and giving,
Reader 2: Being with your family,
Reader 3: Praying for...
Reader 4: Peace on earth, goodwill to all.

Narrator 2: Christmas is more than presents. Christmas is traditions.
Reader 5: Turkey, mashed potatoes, yams and cranberry sauce
Reader 6: Christmas pudding
Reader 7: Eggnog and Christmas nuts
Reader 8: Candy canes
Reader 9: Christmas cake and cookies
Reader 10: Butter tarts and mincemeat tarts
Reader 11: Cookies and a glass of milk for Santa
Reader 1: and carrots for the reindeer.

Narrator 3: Christmas is more than presents. Christmas is special decorations.
Reader 12: Colored light bulbs
Reader 13: Wreaths on doors
Reader 14: Shiny wrapping, ribbons and bows
Reader 15: Holly and mistletoe
Reader 16: Candles lit in windows
Reader 17: Christmas trees
Reader 18: Shining stars
Reader 19: Silver and gold tinsel
Reader 20: Candy canes
Reader 1: Stockings
Reader 22: Christmas tree bulbs
Reader 13: Angels on treetops.

Narrator 4: Christmas is more than presents.
Christmas is singing favorite songs.
Reader 4: Rudolph the Red-nosed Reindeer
Reader 15: Jingle Bells
Reader 16: Silent Night

Reader 17: Winter Wonderland
Reader 20: *(with great enthusiasm)* Candy canes!
Reader 8: We Three Kings
Reader 9: Angels We Have Heard on High
Reader 20: Santa Claus is Coming to Town
Reader 1: Away in the Manger
Reader 7: The First Noel
Reader 16: I Saw Three Ships
Reader 14: It's Beginning To Look a Lot Like Christmas
Reader 20: *(with great enthusiasm)* Candy canes!
Reader 5: We Wish You A Merry Christmas.

Narrator 5: Christmas is more than presents. Christmas is wonderful times.
Reader 6: Making and giving presents to others
Reader 17: Decorating a Christmas tree
Reader 8: Giving to other people in need
Reader 19: Caroling
Reader 20: *(with great enthusiasm)* Candy canes!
Reader 2: Celebrating Jesus' birthday
Reader 1: Being with family
Reader 8: Being with friends
Reader 3: Christmas parties and concerts
Reader 10: Singing around the Christmas tree
Reader 5: Making puzzles
Reader 9: Playing in the snow
Reader 20: *(with great enthusiasm)* Candy canes!
Reader 7: Having fun
Reader 2: Making and baking treats
Reader 6: Singing Christmas songs
Reader 4: Watching happy movies
Reader 20: *(with great enthusiasm)* Candy canes!
Reader 11: Bedtime stories with Mom and Dad.

Narrator 6: Christmas is a time for making memories
Everyone: and Christmas is a time to say thank you. *Thank you!*

Writing Scripts: SCRIPTING STORIES

Children's and teacher's favorite stories and many short stories from anthologies can easily be turned into Readers Theatre scripts for use in the classroom. Once the process has been worked through by the teacher, and students have experienced a variety of scripts, it is a relatively simple task for the students themselves to script a familiar story. The following fairy tale was scripted for Readers Theatre by an eleven-year-old student.

Princess and the Pea *script*

The Princess and the Pea *

Characters	Readers
Narrator 1	_____
Narrator 2	_____
Prince	_____
Girl	_____
Queen	_____
King	_____

Narrator 1: Once upon a time there was a prince who traveled far.

Narrator 2: He traveled far for many months, searching for a princess to marry.

Narrator 1: The prince met many young ladies who said they were princesses,

Narrator 2: but he was not sure they were telling the truth.

Prince: I was most unhappy when I returned to the family castle.

Narrator 1: One night there was a storm,

Narrator 2: a terrible storm!

Queen: With all this thunder and lightning, I'm sure glad we're inside.

Narrator 1: Suddenly, there was a loud knock on the palace door.

Narrator 2: The king answered it.

Narrator 1: Standing at the door was a strange girl.

Girl: Good evening, sir. I've lost my way and I'm cold and wet. May I come in and rest awhile?

King: Of course, my dear, come in at once. You must stay until the storm is over.

Girl: Oh, thank you sir.

Narrator 2: The girl entered and began to dry off and warm up.

Queen: Have some supper, dear. You must be hungry.

Girls: Yes, I am. Thank you, you are so kind.

King: How did you happen to get caught in the storm?

Girl: I was out walking early in the evening. I had wandered far away from the castle (you see, I'm a princess), further than I ever had before, and when the storm happened, I became confused.

* adapted for Readers Theatre by Beth Mole

Reproducible master in Appendix B

Prince: (aside) She says she... I want to believe.

Narrator 1: The queen, who wa...

Narrator 2: She did not tell anyo... slats of the bed.

Queen: On top of the pea I...

Narrator 1: The girl had to climb...

Narrator 2: Next morning the qu...

Queen: Did you sleep well r...

Girl: Oh no, hardly at all...

Queen: Come with me, my d...

Narrator 1: And the queen took...

Queen: Only a real princess... such a pile of pillow...

Narrator 2: The queen explaine...

Queen: You see, I placed a... piled all the other m...

King: ...and of course, as you said, only a real princess would find the bed uncomfortable.

Prince: That was a good test, mother. Thank you. This makes me very happy, as I could wish for nothing more than to have this princess as my wife.

Princess: I am happy, too. I accept your proposal.

Narrator 1: The prince and his newfound princess were married...

Narrator 2: ...and of course they lived happily ever after.

✸ Writing Scripts: SCRIPTING CONVERSATIONS

Conversations are fun to invent. There are many topics which two readers can discuss in single-word and short-sentence conversations. A simple example follows.

Older students may enjoy studying the Abbott and Costello classic, "Who's on First?" This has been reprinted and is available for classroom use in *Skits and Scenes* (1994).

A scripted conversation

Reader 1:	Hi!	**Reader 2:**	Yup.
Reader 2:	Hi.	**Reader 1:**	What was the bonus?
Reader 1:	Going?	**Reader 2:**	Ten bucks.
Reader 2:	Been.	**Reader 1:**	Oh, only ten bucks.
Reader 1:	When?	**Reader 2:**	Yeah.
Reader 2:	Just now.	**Reader 1:**	Well I'm off.
Reader 1:	Why?	**Reader 2:**	Where to?
Reader 2:	It was time.	**Reader 1:**	Just off.
Reader 1:	I wanted to.	**Reader 2:**	Why now?
Reader 2:	Really?	**Reader 1:**	Something to do.
Reader 1:	Yes.	**Reader 2:**	Want a bonus?
Reader 2:	But you said...	**Reader 1:**	Nope.
Reader 1:	Changed my mind.	**Reader 2:**	So, why leave?
Reader 2:	Didn't tell me.	**Reader 1:**	It's time
Reader 1:	Thought you knew!	**Reader 2:**	For what?
Reader 2:	Nope!	**Reader 1:**	A reward.
Reader 1:	What happened?	**Reader 2:**	A reward?
Reader 2:	Nothing.	**Reader 1:**	Yes.
Reader 1:	Nothing?	**Reader 2:**	For what?
Reader 2:	Well...aah...	**Reader 1:**	Listening to you.
Reader 1:	Well what?	**Reader 2:**	Oh.
Reader 2:	I got a bonus.	**Reader 1:**	See ya.
Reader 1:	A bonus!	**Reader 2:**	Yeah, see ya.
Reader 2:	Yeah.		
Reader 1:	Why?		
Reader 2:	For being there.		
Reader 1:	You the only one?		

✸ Writing Scripts: SCRIPTING A PUBLISHED STORY

There are many ways of scripting a short story, chapter, paragraph, or passage. Your choice will be determined by factors such as the age of your students, their experience working in small groups, and the reading abilities of individual readers.

Following is the process:

1. Read the piece.
2. Analyze it in terms of number of characters and amount of dialogue and narration.
3. Script it into parts: one for each character and one for the narrator.

4. Look at the balance between parts. Is there too much narration? Are the character parts too small? Is there a better way for the text to be divided?

5. Make necessary adjustments.

Following is an example of the process one story was subjected to when adapted as a Readers Theatre script:

Draft One

In this example, there is too much direct speech from Grandfather, very little narration, and a small amount of speech for Grandmother. To create a better balance between parts, Grandfather's large parts can be "given" to both the narrator and the grandmother.

Grandfather's Memories

Draft One

For three readers

Narrator:	Over supper Grandfather was still remembering...
Grandfather:	Your grandmother's fresh baking was one of the things that kept us going that winter, but even home baking had its dangers. One afternoon, she was baking pies and she ran out of raisins, so she sent me over to the neighbors' to borrow some. I got bundled up and headed out into the cold. Your grandmother stood in the door waving to me as I went. Without thinking I turned and blew her a kiss. Well, it was so cold that the kiss froze into a solid lump before it got halfway to the house.
Grandmother:	It fetched me such a whack on the forehead that it knocked me senseless for the better part of the day,
Narrator:	said Grandmother.
Grandmother:	I never did get those pies done.
Grandfather:	The cold that winter caused a few problems for the folks in town, too,
Narrator:	said Grandfather.
Grandfather:	It was so cold that when people's breath came out it froze solid. A person had to break off one breath and throw it down on the ground before he could take another one. Soon there were lumps of frozen breath all over the streets. It wasn't long before you could hardly move downtown for the piles of breath every place you turned.

Draft Two

While the second attempt provides for a better balance between readers, there is still enough text to add another reader.

Draft Three

In this draft one narrator is paired with the Grandmother and one narrator is paired with the Grandfather. The narrators tell about the character's words, intents, and actions.

Grandfather's Memories

Draft Two

For three readers

Narrator:	Over supper Grandfather was still remembering...
Grandfather:	Grandmother's fresh baking was one of the things that kept us going that winter.
Grandmother:	But even home baking had its dangers. One afternoon, I was baking pies and I ran out of raisins.
Grandfather:	She sent me over to the neighbors' to borrow some.
Grandmother:	He got bundled up and headed out into the cold.
Grandfather:	She stood in the door waving to me as I went. Without thinking I turned and blew her a kiss.
Grandmother:	Well, it was so cold that the kiss froze into a solid lump before it got halfway to the house.
Grandfather:	It fetched her such a whack on the forehead that it knocked her senseless for the better part of the day.
Grandmother:	I never did get those pies done.
Narrator:	The cold that winter caused a few problems for the folks in town too.
Grandfather:	It was so cold that when people's breath came out it froze solid.
Grandmother:	A person had to break off one breath and throw it down on the ground before he could take another one.
Narrator:	Soon there were lumps of frozen breath all over the streets.
Grandfather:	It wasn't long before you could hardly move downtown for the piles of breath every place you turned.

Grandfather's M...

Draft Three

For four readers

Narrator 1:	Over supper Grandfather was still remembering...
Narrator 2:	about Grandmother's fresh baking.
Grandfather:	It was one of the things that kept us going that winter.
Grandmother:	But even home baking had its dangers,
Narrator 2:	Grandmother continued.
Grandmother:	One afternoon, I was baking pies...
Grandfather:	...and she ran out of raisins,
Narrator 1:	Grandfather interrupted.
Grandfather:	She sent me over to the neighbors' to borrow some.
Narrator 1:	He got bundled up and headed out into the cold.
Narrator 2:	She stood in the door and waved to him as he went.
Grandfather:	Without thinking I turned and blew her a kiss.
Grandmother:	Well, it was so cold that the kiss froze into a solid lump
Narrator 1:	before it got halfway to the house.
Narrator 2:	It fetched her such a whack on the forehead
Grandmother:	that it knocked me senseless for the better part of the day.
Grandfather:	She never did get those pies done,
Narrator 1:	chimed in Grandfather.
Narrator 2:	The cold that winter caused a few problems for the folks in town, too.
Narrator 1:	It was so cold that when people's breath came out it froze solid.
Narrator 2:	A person had to break off one breath and throw it down on the ground
Narrator 1:	before he could take another one.
Grandmother:	Soon there were lumps of frozen breath all over the streets,
Narrator 2:	added Grandmother.
Narrator 1:	It wasn't long before you could hardly move downtown
Grandfather:	for the piles of breath every place you turned.

Grandfather's Memories *

Final Draft

For four readers

Narrator 1:	Over supper Grandfather was still remembering...
Grandfather:	*Hmmm, your grandmother's fresh baking...that was one of the things that kept us going that winter,*
Narrator 1:	*he recalled.*
Grandmother:	But even home baking had its dangers,
Narrator 2:	Grandmother continued.
Grandmother:	One afternoon I was baking pies...
Grandfather:	and she ran out of raisins,
Narrator 1:	Grandfather interrupted.
Narrator 1:	*Grandfather was sent to the neighbors' to borrow some.*
Grandmother:	Get bundled up before you head out into the cold,
Narrator 2:	*Grandmother shivered as she remembered.*
Grandfather:	*You bet,*
Narrator 1:	*replied Grandfather.*
Grandfather:	*She stood in the door waving to me*
Narrator 1:	*Grandfather told how he left and then said*
Grandfather:	*Of course without thinking I turned and blew her a kiss.*
Narrator 1:	*Grandfather wasn't thinking when he blew the kiss!*
Narrator 2:	*Because of the severe cold...*
All:	*How cold?*
Grandmother:	So cold that the kiss froze into a solid lump
Grandfather:	before it got halfway to the house.
Narrator 1:	*added Grandfather.*
Narrator 2:	*That solid kiss hit Grandmother full force...*
All:	*Whack!*

*adapted from Cold Night, Brittle Light, by Richard Thompson, © 1994, Orca Book Publishers.

Final Draft

This script can be further enhanced by adding more text, expressions, or dialogue. This has been done in the next example. Additions are in italics.

Grandmother:	*Right on my forehead.*
Narrator 2:	It knocked Grandmother senseless
Grandmother:	for the better part of the day
Narrator 2:	*and then she added*
Grandmother:	I never did get those pies done.
Narrator 1:	The cold that winter caused a few problems
Narrator 2:	for the folks in town, too.
Grandfather:	It was so cold
All:	*How cold?*
Narrator 1:	*And Grandfather responded*
Grandfather:	that when people's breath came out it froze solid
Narrator 2:	*Grandmother added*
Grandmother:	A person had to break off one breath and throw it down on the ground before he could take another one.
Narrator 1:	Lumps of frozen breath all over the streets.
Grandfather:	It wasn't long before you could hardly move downtown
Grandmother:	for the piles of breath every place you turned.

STAGING

Performing a Readers Theatre script for an audience is not a priority; it is an option. Staging is simple: unlike conventional theatre production, which incorporates the scenery, costumes and props, Readers Theatre characters rely on simple, common items to help them communicate their roles. Music stands support the scripts. Benches, stools, chairs, risers, and boxes provide different levels for both standing and sitting. A cape or hat may symbolize a particular character. Remember that simplicity of the staging means an easy, unfettered production. This chapter explores some staging considerations for Readers Theatre productions.

Staging:

✹ *Staging:* SIMPLE READERS THEATRE

Simple staging restricts readers to basic moves, thus allowing them to focus on their reading.

1. Select a script or story.
2. After reviewing their parts, have readers sit in a circle.
3. Rehearse reading, focusing on character and expression.
4. When ready, arrange music stands in a "power-of-character" position. This involves placing the main character downstage center and the lesser characters stage right, stage left, or further upstage. Readers located upstage need to be at a higher level. This can be achieved either by lowering the forward readers (by having them sit on the floor or on chairs) or raising the upstage readers (by having them stand on the floor, risers, or chairs).

Following is a script employing simple staging, based on Shel Silverstein's "Ladies First."

Detail of script showing simple staging diagram

Ladies First

by Shel Silverstein
Adapted for Readers Theatre

Roles for Readers	Student Names
Narrator 1	_____
Narrator 2	_____
Lady	_____
Chief Tiger	_____
Tigers (2 or 3)	_____
	_____
	_____

Enter from stage right, carrying scripts under right arm, Narrator 2 leads, followed by Tiger 2, Chief Tiger, Tiger 1, Lady, Narrator 1. All take positions behind their music stands. Three tigers lower their heads to show they are out of the scene.

Narrators use audience focus, characters use offstage focus.

Suggested Staging

N1 T1 CT L T2 N2

Audience

Readers enter from stage right, with scripts placed under their right arms. When in position behind music stands, Narrator 1 gives the signal by placing the script on the music stand. Three tigers lower their heads (which signals they are out of the action). *Simple version*

Narrator 2:	Ladies First, by Shel Silverstein.
Narrator 1:	Did you hear the one about the little girl who was the "tender, sweet young thing"? Well, that's the way she thought of herself.
Narrator 2:	And this tender sweet young thing spent a great deal of time just looking in the mirror, saying:
Lady:	(*indicates each item by pointing*) I am a real little lady. Anybody could tell that. I wear lovely, starched cotton dresses with matching ribbons in my lovely, curly locks. I wear clean white socks and black, shiny patent-leather shoes, and I always put just a dab of perfume behind my ear.
Narrator 2:	When she was at the end of the lunch line in school all she had to say was...
Lady:	Ladies first, ladies first...
Narrator 1:	and she'd get right up to the front of the line. (*Lady smiles victoriously*)
Narrator 2:	Well, her life went on like that for quite a while and she wound up having a pretty good time—you know—admiring herself in mirrors, always getting to be first in line, and stuff like that.
Narrator 1:	And then one day, she went exploring with a whole group of other people through the wilds of a deep and beastly jungle. As she went along through the tangled trails and prickly vines, she would say things like:
Lady:	(*indicates each item by pointing*) I have got to be careful of my lovely dress and my nice white socks and my shiny, shiny shoes and my curly, curly locks. So would somebody please clear the way for me?
Narrator 1:	And they did.
Narrator 2:	Or sometimes she'd say...
Lady:	What-do-you-mean there aren't enough mangoes to go around, and I'll have to share my mango—because I was the last one across the icky river full of crocodiles and snakes?
Lady:	No matter how last I am, it's still "Ladies first, ladies first", so (*harshly*) hand over a whole mango, (*softly, pleasantly*) please!!!
Narrator 2:	And they did.
Narrator 1:	Well then, guess what happened?

Narrator 2:	Suddenly the exploring party was seized (*Tigers lift heads and sniff around*) by the tigers and dragged back to their lair, where the tigers sniffed around, trying to decide what would make the best dinner.
Chief Tiger:	How about this one? (*Focus audience left*)
Tigers:	Naah, too bony...
Chief Tiger:	What about this one? (*Focus audience right*)
Tigers:	Uh-unh, meaty, but too muscle-y.
Chief Tiger:	Oh, for heaven's sake, don't take all night.
Narrator 2:	said the Chief Tiger.
Chief Tiger:	I never saw such a pack of picky eaters! How about this one (*focus down in front of Lady*) then? It looks tender, and smells nice. In fact, I never saw anything quite like this before. I wonder what it is?
Lady:	I am a sweet young thing (*focus up in front of Chief Tiger*).
Narrator 1:	She said
Chief Tiger:	Oh, far out!
Narrator 2:	said the Tiger Chief.
Lady:	I'm also a little lady. You should know that by my lovely clothes and my lovely smell. And if it's all the same to you, Tiger Tweetie, I wish you'd (*harshly*) stop licking me and untie me this instant. (*Pleasantly*) My dress is getting mussed.
Chief Tiger:	Yes...Well, as a matter of fact, we were all just trying to decide who to untie first.
Lady:	Ladies first! Ladies first!
Narrator 1:	she said,
Narrator 2:	and so she was. (*Lady lowers head to be out of scene*)
All Tigers:	AND MIGHTY TASTY, TOO !!!

(*Lady lifts head and all readers place scripts under right arm and turn to face stage right, led off by Narrator 1, the others follow in this order: Narrator 1, Tiger 1, Chief Tiger, Lady, Tiger 2, and Narrator 2*)

✿ *Staging:* STAGED READERS THEATRE

Staged Readers Theatre is a more advanced form of presenting Readers Theatre, in which movements of the readers (exits, entrances, and gestures) play an important part in the presentation. Although the focus is still mainly on the reading, exits, entrances, turns, and gestures contribute to the development of character and expression.

1. Choose a script.

2. Students sort out parts with teacher's help.

3. Read the script for understanding several times, together and independently.

4. Decide on the staging—levels, positions of characters, placement of narrators, types of focus (onstage or offstage)—and whether music stands will be used by none, some, or all.

Staging illustrations for more advanced version

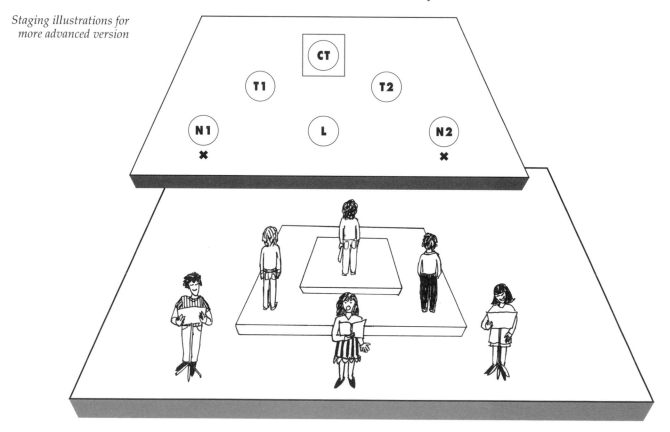

5. Formalize the beginning of the performance—walking on stage in a line, all carrying scripts in the same way. Take the lead from the last in line who, when in position gives the signal for the start (for example, placing script in reading position). Characters who are not yet part of the performance turn their backs to the audience.

6. After the performance, readers exit the stage, taking their lead from the same reader who started them. They all place their scripts under their right arm (exit stage position), turn and face the same way, and walk from the stage.

Staged Readers Theatre is most useful for elementary classrooms. Limited physical action is encouraged. Visual and auditory elements are included, and the piece begins with a formal entrance and ends with a formal exit. Props and other equipment are not encouraged; instead scripts may be used to suggest objects.

Staged version

Ladies First

by Shel Silverstein
Adapted for Readers Theatre

Roles for Readers	Student Names
Narrator 1	_____
Narrator 2	_____
Lady	_____
Chief Tiger	_____
Tigers (2 or 3)	_____
	_____
	_____
	_____

Formal entrance from stage right with scripts under right arms in the following order: Narrator 2, Tiger 2, Chief Tiger, Tiger 1, Lady, Narrator 1.

Chief Tiger stands on chair at center stage. Other tigers on floor flanking Chief. Narrator 1 and Narrator 2 behind music stands. All face front until Narrator 1 removes script to reading position. Other characters follow and tigers right about turn to have their backs to the audience.

Suggested Staging

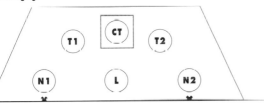

Narrator 2	Ladies First, by Shel Silverstein.

(Audience eye contact)

Narrator 1:	(*Addressing Narrator 2 on stage left*) Did you hear the one about the little girl who was the "tender sweet young thing"? (*Addresses audience*) Well, that's the way she thought of herself.
Narrator 2:	(*Addressing audience*) And this tender sweet young thing spent a great deal of time just looking in the mirror, saying:
Lady:	I am a *real* little lady. Anybody could tell that. (*Gestures to dress*) I wear lovely starched cotton dresses with matching (*flicks hair*) ribbons in my lovely, curly locks. I wear clean white (*indicate feet*) socks and black, shiny patent-leather shoes and I always (*dab perfume*) put just a dab of perfume behind each ear.
Narrator 2:	When she was at the end of the lunch line in school all she had to say was...
Lady:	(*Politely*) Ladies first, (*harshly*) ladies first (*repeat line with different emphasis*),
Narrator 1:	and she'd get right up to the front of the line (*Lady shows how pleased she is*).
Narrator 2:	Well, her life went on like that for quite a while and she wound up having a pretty good time (*Lady looks smug*)—you know—(*Lady mimes these actions*) admiring herself in mirrors, always getting to be first in line, and stuff like that...
Narrator 1:	and then one day, she went exploring with a whole group of other people through the wilds of a (*Lady shows distaste*) deep and beastly jungle. As she went along through the tangled trails and prickly vines, she would say things like:
Lady:	(*Indicating each*) I have got to be careful of my lovely dress and my nice white socks and my shiny, shiny shoes and my curly, curly locks. So would somebody (*harshly*) **please** (*nicely*) clear the way for me?
Narrator 1:	And they did.
Narrator 2:	Or sometimes she'd say:
Lady:	What-do-you-mean there aren't enough mangoes to go around, and I'll have to share my mango—because I was the last one across that icky river full of crocodiles and snakes? No matter how last I am, it's still "Ladies first, (*harshly*)ladies first", (*Point script towards audience*) so (*sternly*) hand over a whole mango, (*pleasantly*) please!!!
Narrator 2:	and they did.
Narrator 1:	Well then, guess what happened?

Narrator 2:	Suddenly the exploring party was seized (*Tigers turn right to face front*) by the tigers and dragged back to their lair, where the tigers sniffed (*Tigers sniff air and make hungry, lip-smacking sounds*) around, trying to decide what would make the best dinner.
Chief Tiger:	How about this one (*pointing off stage left to a person in the audience*)?
Narrator 1:	said the Chief tiger
Tigers:	(*Turning towards the selected audience member*) Naah, too bony...
Chief Tiger:	What about this one (*pointing off stage right to another audience member*)?
Tigers:	(*Turning towards the selected member of the audience*) Uh-unh, meaty, but too muscle-y.
Chief Tiger:	I never saw such a pack of picky eaters! How about this one (*looking down and pointing to a person in the front row*) then? It looks tender, (*sniffing and licking*) and smells nice. In fact, I never saw anything quite like this before. I wonder what it is.
Lady:	(*Looking towards ceiling above the position pointed to by the chief tiger*) I am a sweet young thing,
Narrator 1:	she said.
Chief Tiger:	Oh, far out!
Narrator 2:	said the Tiger chief.
Lady:	I'm also a little lady. You should know that by my lovely clothes and my lovely smell. And if it's all the same to you, Tiger Tweetie, I wish you'd (*sternly*) stop licking me and untie me, this instant. (*Pleasantly*) My dress is getting mussed.
Chief Tiger:	Yes...Well, as a matter of fact, we were all just trying to decide who to untie first.
Lady:	Ladies first! (*Emphasize ladies in the repeated line*) Ladies first!
Narrator 1:	she said.
Narrator 2:	And so she was! (*Lady turns her back towards the audience*)
All Tigers:	AND MIGHTY TASTY, TOO!

Pause for count of three, then Lady turns front.

All place scripts under right arms, then all turn stage right and, led by N1, walk off stage in the following order: N1, Tiger 1, Lady, Chief Tiger, Tiger 2, and Narrator 2.

🧩 *Staging:* BLOCKING

Blocking refers to the position of the readers on stage and any moves they make during the performance. An odd number of performers is easier to deal with than an even number. Stools, chairs, and benches are used to vary the height of the characters. Tiers, risers, or benches are used once the number of performers exceeds ten.

Blocking diagrams

Two performers
a) Both seated, pointing, offstage focus

b) Both standing, onstage focus

R1 R2

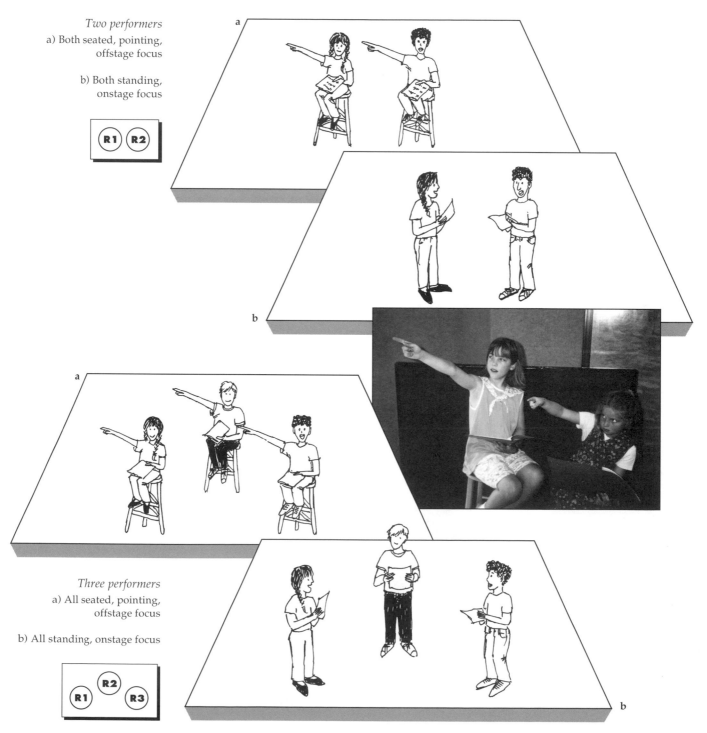

Three performers
a) All seated, pointing, offstage focus

b) All standing, onstage focus

R2
R1 R3

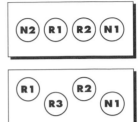

Four performers

a) Staged Readers Theatre, offstage focus

b) Staged Readers Theatre, offstage focus

Four performers

c) Simple Readers Theatre, offstage focus, all readers seated

d) Same setup as above, but all performers have turned to make a "totem pole." Offstage focus for all.

Five performers
a) Staged Readers Theatre, onstage focus for two readers

b) Staged Readers Theatre, onstage focus for N1, R1, R2, R3, but offstage focus for R4

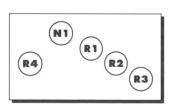

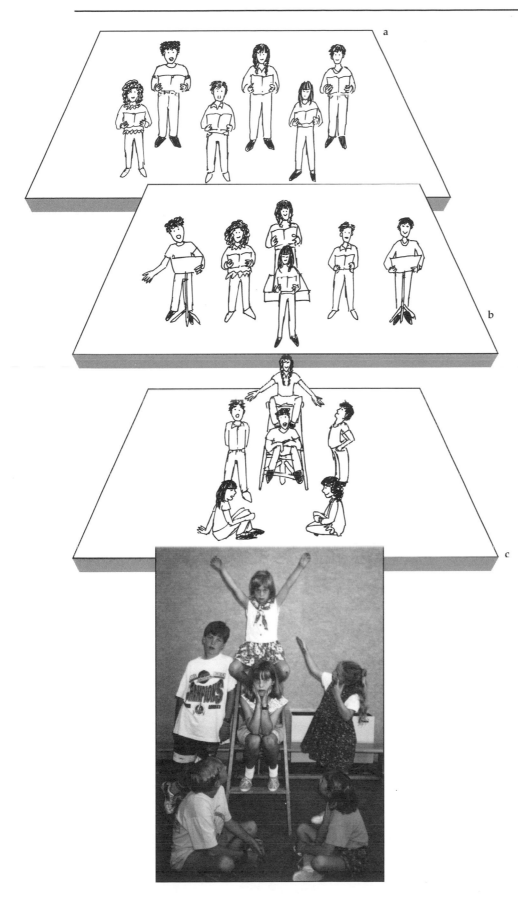

Six performers

a) Simple Readers Theatre, offstage focus

b) Staged Readers Theatre, audience focus for narrators, offstage for other performers

c) Staged Readers Theatre, using a variety of heights to keep the staging area small. Readers use onstage focus, narrators use offstage focus. Lines are memorized.

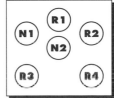

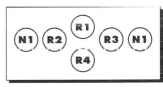

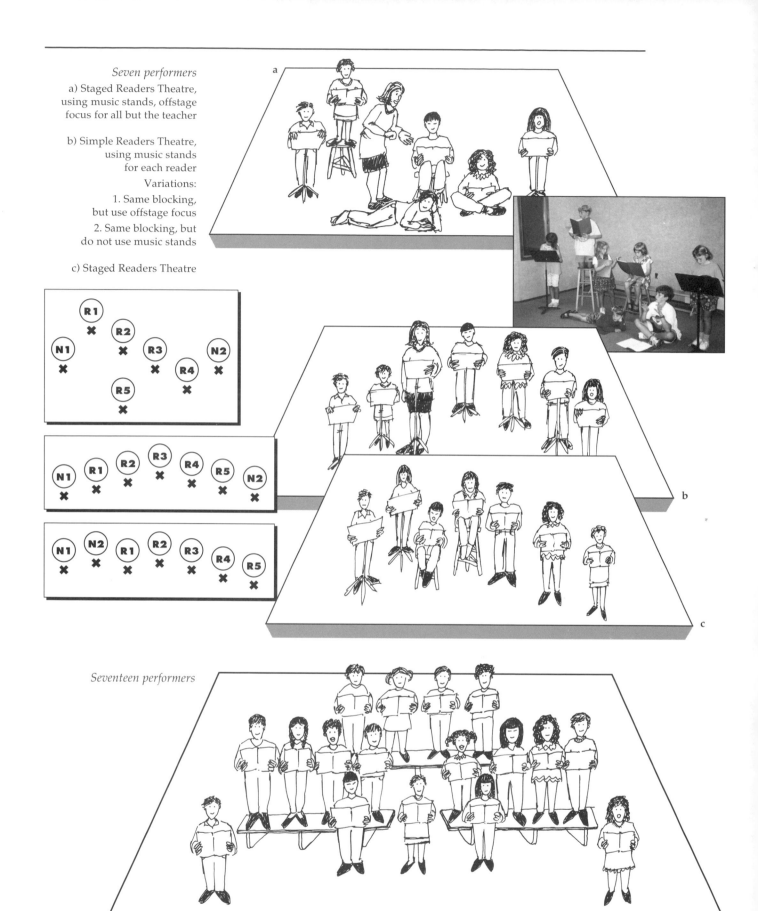

Seven performers

a) Staged Readers Theatre, using music stands, offstage focus for all but the teacher

b) Simple Readers Theatre, using music stands for each reader
Variations:
1. Same blocking, but use offstage focus
2. Same blocking, but do not use music stands

c) Staged Readers Theatre

Seventeen performers

CONNECTING CURRICULUM WITH READERS THEATRE

Although you may already be using Readers Theatre successfully in your classrooms, teachers always welcome more ideas. The purpose of this section is to provide starting structures that can help you

- ☛ create Readers Theatre from events that take place in your classroom every day
- ☛ involve children in the planning stages
- ☛ custom design Readers Theatre for you and your students

Connecting Curriculum With Readers Theatre:

✹ *Connecting Curriculum:* ENDING A THEME

One class had been studying the seashore. They went on a field trip, they studied beaches and plant life, they observed tidal pools and sea life in nature, they read books about the sea and read stories with sea settings. As a closing event they prepared a Readers Theatre script. They shared it with one another as they practiced, and then with the whole school at assembly. Following is the process they used:

1. The teacher worked with her students to create a giant web of everything they had learned.

2. The class examined the web and the ideas it represented. They categorized the ideas into major groups.

3. They chose a script structure (see page 33).

4. They wrote the script.

5. They practiced and presented their Readers Theatre script to an audience.

Script based on seashore theme

Seashore

Roles for Readers	Student Names
Reader 1	_____
Reader 2	_____
Reader 3	_____
Reader 4	_____
Reader 5	_____

Suggested Staging

R1 R2 R3 R4 R5

Audience

Reader 3: waves lapping,
Reader 2: seabirds calling.

Reader 1: What do you smell at the seashore?
Reader 3: Salty air,
Reader 4: seaweed,
Reader 5: suntan lotion,
Reader 2: smoke from the fire.

Reader 5: I like to swim with the incoming tide.
Reader 3: I like to relax in the sun.
Reader 1: I like to sleep on the beach logs.
Reader 2: I like to read.
Reader 4: I like to look for shells.
Reader 2: I like to listen to the water lapping.
Reader 3: I like to explore.
Reader 5: I like to snorkel.
Reader 1: I like to play volleyball on the sand.
Reader 4: I like to put my ear to the conch shell.

All: We hear the seashore calling.

Reader 1: What can you see at the seashore?
Reader 2: Clams squirting,
Reader 3: crabs scuttling,
Reader 4: seagulls scrapping,
Reader 5: children swimming.

Reader 1: What can you hear at the seashore?
Reader 2: Surf crashing,
Reader 5: children laughing,

Reproducible master in Appendix B

✦ *Connecting Curriculum:* INTRODUCING A TOPIC IN SOCIAL STUDIES

Three teachers created an original script to introduce social studies concepts, including names and locations of six continents, major oceans, the ten provinces and two territories of Canada, facts about British Columbia, and differences between urban and rural communities. This encouraged children to think about where they live in relationship to the entire world. Try this:

1. Select or write a script that introduces the key concepts.

2. Make multiple copies of the script, one for each student.

3. Read the script aloud, with students following along silently.

4. Read the script aloud together.

5. Divide roles among children in the class (two or more children can combine their voices and be a single character). Children highlight their role with a highlighting pen and then work together to prepare the script for presentation.

6. Present to own class, then to other classes.

A Visitor from Space

Written and adapted for Readers Theatre by
Rosemary Ronalds, Teri Rychlik, and Sharon Niddrie

Social studies script

Narrator:	Somewhere from a far-off planet out in space, an alien was sent on a *very important* mission...As the alien slowly opened the spaceship door and looked out, he wondered where he could be.
Alien:	Where in the universe am I?
Narrator:	Peeking out from behind a tree was a little person. Timidly the child walked closer to the alien.
Student:	You're on the planet Earth.
Alien:	Good. You must be Tom. I was sent to Earth to visit Tom. Did you send us a message on your computer?
Narrator:	The student shook his head and said,
Student:	I'm not Tom! Where does he live?
Alien:	Well, on Earth of course.
Narrator:	said the alien.
Student:	But there's six continents and billions of people on earth!
Alien:	Whaddya mean, continents?
Student:	You know, those big chunks of land separated by oceans.
Alien:	Six of them you say?
Narrator:	asked the alien, scratching his head.
Student:	Yeah. Asia, Europe, North America, South America, Africa...
Alien:	Wait, North America rings a bell.
Narrator:	Now the alien and the student began to get excited.
Student:	Good. Now, where in North America?
Alien:	Who knows? What choice do I have?
Narrator:	The student began to name the countries.
Student:	United States, Canada or Mexico.
Narrator:	The alien looked puzzled.
Alien:	Huh? Aren't there any more?
Student:	Nope. That's it. That's all—only three countries in North America,
Narrator:	said the student with a firm nod of his head.
Alien:	Wait... the country with bumpy hills?
Narrator:	The student smiled and answered,

Student:	You mean the Rocky Mountains?
Alien:	Yeah. That's it! The Rocky Mountains. The northern part,
Narrator:	said the alien, nodding excitedly.
Student:	Then it's Canada. Canada has Rockies.
Narrator:	The alien thinks for a moment, then says,
Alien:	Then I am in the right place. Earth...North America...Canada...So, where's Tom?
Narrator:	The student shakes his head and says,
Student:	Canada's big, too. It has ten provinces and two territories—different shapes and different sizes.
Alien:	Hmm. Provinces...any choices here?
Narrator:	The student begins to name the provinces.
Student:	Well, there's Ontario, Manitoba, Alberta, British Columbia, Quebec...
Alien:	That's it!
Narrator:	exclaimed the alien.
Student:	You mean Quebec?
Alien:	No, British Columbia. Now we're cooking. Tom's getting closer...
Narrator:	Again the student shakes his head.
Student:	Good grief. Don't you know how big British Columbia is?
Narrator:	The alien shook his head sheepishly
Student:	You'll have to name a city.
Alien:	Is...is...is a city the same as an island?
Narrator:	asked the very confused alien.
Student:	Sheesh!
Narrator:	the student said, as he threw his hands up in the air.
Student:	This is very confusing...but our city is on an island.
Narrator:	The poor alien was not too sure what to ask next.
Alien:	City?
Student:	You know, some cities like—my grandma lives in Vancouver, my auntie lives in Kelowna, our capital is Victoria...and I live in Nanaimo.
Narrator:	Suddenly the alien reached down into his pocket and pulled out a piece of paper...
Alien:	*(Looks at the paper)* So I am in the right place! TOOOOOOOOOOOOM...

Connecting Curriculum With Readers Theatre **55**

❧ *Connecting Curriculum:* TEACHING A CONCEPT IN SCIENCE

Before asking students to perform a science experiment, they need to become familiar with its various components. One teacher created Readers Theatre scripts to introduce the key scientific processes, including purpose, materials, observations, method, and conclusion.

1. Make multiple copies of the script—one for each student. (In the case of the following set of scripts there are a total of eighteen readers. Since most classes have more than eighteen students you need to assign two readers to some of the roles so every student is involved. You may choose to assign a less able reader with a more able one or a student with a quiet voice with another child to ensure volume.)

2. Everyone reads through the scripts silently.

3. Roles are assigned or selected.

Science scripts

4. Each student highlights their part so it will be easy to track as they read.

5. Students practice their script for one another and for other groups. (Consider providing a video camera so students can videotape their performance and receive instant feedback on its effectiveness.)

6. Students perform for each other.

This activity is a wonderfully effective launch for a unit about science experiments. These scripts could also be used as a opening for a school-wide science fair. Writing scripts such as these is an effective culminating activity.

Purpose

Roles for Readers   **Student Names**

Reader 1   _____

Reader 2   _____

Reader 3   _____

Suggested Staging

Audience

Reader 1:	Science!
Reader 2:	Experiments!
Reader 3:	Purpose!
Reader 1:	But what is a purpose?
Reader 2:	A reason.
Reader 3:	A question; looking for an answer.
Reader 2:	A hypothesis; a guess.
Reader 1:	But, why have a purpose?
Reader 3:	To guide, explore, investigate.
Reader 2:	To examine, search.
Reader 3:	Okay, a purpose is...
Reader 2:	a statement that sets the stage for the experiment!
Reader 1:	Example?
Reader 3:	To observe gas bubbles being pushed out of a soda by particles of salt
Reader 1:	I got it!...Do you?
Reader 2:	Science!
Reader 3:	Experiments!
Reader 1:	Purpose!
All:	Fun!

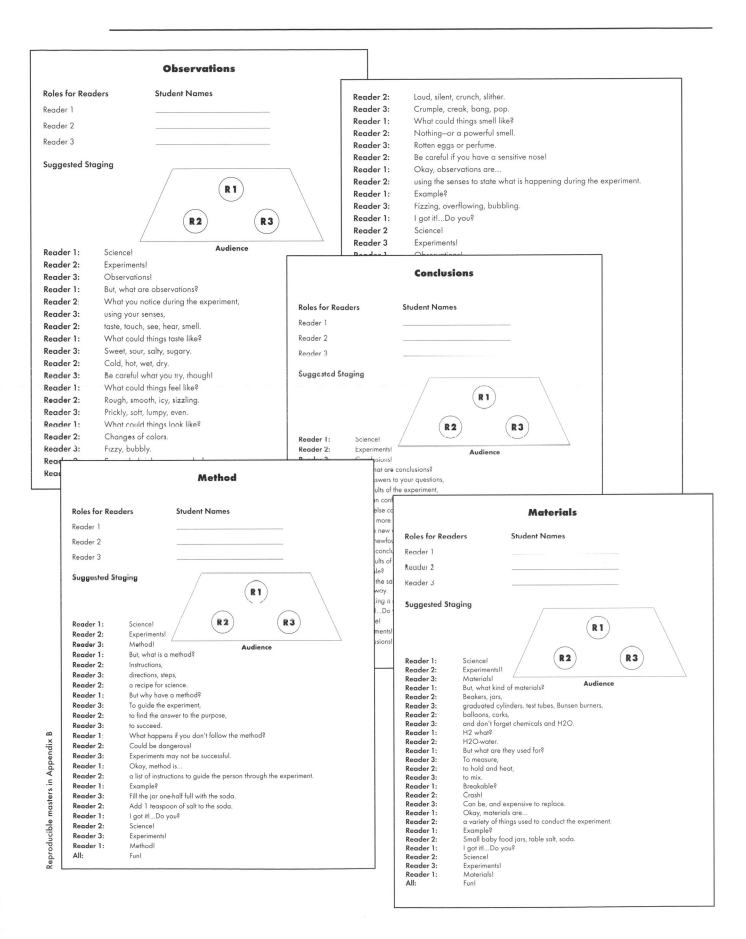

Observations

Roles for Readers	Student Names
Reader 1	_____
Reader 2	_____
Reader 3	_____

Suggested Staging

Audience

Reader 1:	Science!
Reader 2:	Experiments!
Reader 3:	Observations!
Reader 1:	But, what are observations?
Reader 2:	What you notice during the experiment,
Reader 3:	using your senses,
Reader 2:	taste, touch, see, hear, smell.
Reader 1:	What could things taste like?
Reader 3:	Sweet, sour, salty, sugary.
Reader 2:	Cold, hot, wet, dry.
Reader 3:	Be careful what you try, though!
Reader 1:	What could things feel like?
Reader 2:	Rough, smooth, icy, sizzling.
Reader 3:	Prickly, soft, lumpy, even.
Reader 1:	What could things look like?
Reader 2:	Changes of colors.
Reader 3:	Fizzy, bubbly.

Reader 2:	Loud, silent, crunch, slither.
Reader 3:	Crumple, creak, bang, pop.
Reader 1:	What could things smell like?
Reader 2:	Nothing—or a powerful smell.
Reader 3:	Rotten eggs or perfume.
Reader 2:	Be careful if you have a sensitive nose!
Reader 1:	Okay, observations are...
Reader 2:	using the senses to state what is happening during the experiment.
Reader 1:	Example?
Reader 3:	Fizzing, overflowing, bubbling.
Reader 1:	I got it!...Do you?
Reader 2	Science!
Reader 3	Experiments!
Reader 1	Observations!

Conclusions

Roles for Readers	Student Names
Reader 1	_____
Reader 2	_____
Reader 3	_____

Suggested Staging

Audience

Reader 1:	Science!
Reader 2:	Experiments!
Reader 3:	Conclusions!

(what are conclusions?
answers to your questions,
results of the experiment,
...n confi...
else c...
...more
...o new
...ewfou...
...conclu...
...ults of
...le?
...the sa...
...way.
...ting a
...d...Do...
...ments!
...sions!)

Method

Roles for Readers	Student Names
Reader 1	_____
Reader 2	_____
Reader 3	_____

Suggested Staging

Audience

Reader 1:	Science!
Reader 2:	Experiments!
Reader 3:	Method!
Reader 1:	But, what is a method?
Reader 2:	Instructions,
Reader 3:	directions, steps,
Reader 2:	a recipe for science.
Reader 1:	But why have a method?
Reader 3:	To guide the experiment,
Reader 2:	to find the answer to the purpose,
Reader 3:	to succeed.
Reader 1:	What happens if you don't follow the method?
Reader 2:	Could be dangerous!
Reader 3:	Experiments may not be successful.
Reader 1:	Okay, method is...
Reader 2:	a list of instructions to guide the person through the experiment.
Reader 1:	Example?
Reader 3:	Fill the jar one-half full with the soda.
Reader 2:	Add 1 teaspoon of salt to the soda.
Reader 1:	I got it!...Do you?
Reader 2:	Science!
Reader 3:	Experiments!
Reader 1:	Method!
All:	Fun!

Materials

Roles for Readers	Student Names
Reader 1	_____
Reader 2	_____
Reader 3	_____

Suggested Staging

Audience

Reader 1:	Science!
Reader 2:	Experiments!!
Reader 3:	Materials!
Reader 1:	But, what kind of materials?
Reader 2:	Beakers, jars,
Reader 3:	graduated cylinders, test tubes, Bunsen burners,
Reader 2:	balloons, corks,
Reader 3:	and don't forget chemicals and H2O.
Reader 1:	H2 what?
Reader 2:	H2O-water.
Reader 1:	But what are they used for?
Reader 3:	To measure,
Reader 2:	to hold and heat,
Reader 3:	to mix.
Reader 1:	Breakable?
Reader 2:	Crash!
Reader 3:	Can be, and expensive to replace.
Reader 1:	Okay, materials are...
Reader 2:	a variety of things used to conduct the experiment.
Reader 1:	Example?
Reader 2:	Small baby food jars, table salt, soda.
Reader 1:	I got it!...Do you?
Reader 2:	Science!
Reader 3:	Experiments!
Reader 1:	Materials!
All:	Fun!

Reproducible masters in Appendix B

Two teachers decided they could introduce students to the library using Readers Theatre. They worked together to prepare a script using the script-building steps outlined on page 33. They presented the script to their students, using it to focus a discussion about the library.

Library script

Introducing the Library

Written and adapted for Readers Theatre by
Sue Postans and Cindy Lowry

Roles for Readers   **Student Names**

Reader 1   _____

Reader 2   _____

Librarian   _____

Suggested Staging

R1   R2   L

Audience

Librarian:	Shhh!
Reader 2:	Shhh!
All:	SHHH!
Reader 1:	We're in the library...
Librarian:	Books, films, videos...
Reader 2:	Pictures, vertical files, computers...
Reader 1:	Card catalogue!
Reader 2:	Dewey Decimal!
Reader 1:	Due?
Librarian:	Overdue.
Reader 1:	It's due today.
Reader 2:	Report due tomorrow...
Reader 1:	How DO I find...?
Reader 2:	WHERE do I find...?

Reader 1:	Where's Waldo?
Librarian:	Magazines...
Reader 1:	National Geographic...
Reader 2:	Owl!
Librarian:	Sports Illustrated?
Reader 1:	Books!
Reader 2:	Fantasy, mystery, romance, fairy tales!
Reader 1:	Poetry, novels, stories!
Librarian:	FICTION!
Reader 2:	Biography, animals, space,
Reader 1:	dinosaurs, jokes, history,
Librarian:	nonfiction.
Reader 2:	It's raining outside.
Librarian:	Games, readings, story times!
Reader 1:	Time out!
Librarian:	It's sunny. Go outside.
Reader 1:	But Mrs. Library...
Librarian:	Outside!
Reader 1:	Awwww!
Reader 2:	School's closed!
Reader 1:	Oh no!
Reader 2:	Wait a minute.
Reader 1 & 2:	We can go to the public library!

Reproducible master in Appendix B

✦ *Connecting Curriculum:* EXPLAINING KEY MUSIC CONCEPTS

One teacher, looking for an effective way to introduce six basic components of music—beat, rhythm, melody, timbre, texture, and form—wrote this Readers Theatre script, in which two children find an old jukebox and plug it in. It teaches the basic components of music and includes scripting and staging.

The music teacher first selected a class of older students to perform this for younger students. Later in the year she had the younger classes perform it for their parents on a musical evening.

The Music Machine

Written and adapted for Readers Theatre by Sue Postans

Roles for Readers	Student Names
Narrator 1	_____
Narrator 2	_____
Jukebox	_____
Girl	_____
Boy	_____

(To begin, there could be strains of "The Music Goes Round and Round" played faintly.)

Narrator 1: Once upon a time there was an old jukebox sitting in the back corner of a cobwebby old garage. For many years it sat there silently, until one day a group of children playing nearby noticed that the door was open just a bit. Being well-brought up children, they knew to respect private property and never go into a building uninvited, but somehow they knew it would be all right to go into this particular place. They carefully squeezed through the doorway and then saw the old jukebox.

Girl: What's that?

Boy: An old jukebox.

Girl: What's an old jukebox?

Boy: Oh, you know. It's a machine that plays music w

Girl: A music machine?

Narrator 2: They went closer, curious to see more.

Boy: Maybe if we plug it in, it will play for us.

Narrator 1: One of them found the plug.

Narrator 2: One of them found an electrical outlet.

Narrator 1: They plugged in the jukebox.

Narrator 1: and waited...

Narrator 2: and waited...

Narrator 1: nothing happened.

Girl: We have to turn it on, dude!

Narrator 2: They found a switch on the back of the jukebox

Jukebox: Hi. I'm a magic music machine. I don't just play

Boy: Sounds just like my music teacher.

Girl: Shhh!

Music script

Boy: What is music, Mr. Machine?

Jukebox: Music is beat, melody, rhythm, texture, form and timbre.

Girl: You're right, that sounds just like Mrs. Postans!

Jukebox: Watch and listen!

Narrator 1: The jukebox seemed to glow in the darkened garage. Suddenly a picture formed on its glass front.

Boy: Just like a TV!

Girl: Hey, isn't that a heart?

Jukebox: You're right. The basis of all music is beat, and like your heart, it just keeps on going. It may be fast, like when you have run a race, or it may be slow, like when you wake up from a nap, but it keeps on going. What happens if your heart stops beating?

Boy: You die.

Jukebox: In other words, you stop, too, right? Well, when beat stops, so does the music. I think of the beat as walking.

Girl: What else is in music?

Jukebox: Rhythm!

Girl: How do you spell that?

Boy: R-H-Y-T-H-M.

Jukebox: Right. Now rap it.

Girl: R-H-Y...T-H-M! (Can go on for a while. Then add)

Boy: BEAT-BEAT-BEAT-BEAT (Do together a few times)

Jukebox: Rhythm is the long and short of your sound. You might say that the beat does the [...] jukebox's screen.

[...] The beat does the walking and [...] the other on the stocking.

[...] hearing?

[...] sometimes I hum a happy tune.

[...] and it's the high and low of music, [...] higher and lower.

[...] and talk.

[...] to my pictures of music. There, now [...] and valleys.

[...] 's okay. What happens when a

Boy: We walk and talk and go up and down hills together?

Jukebox: Yes. But does your friend walk the same or sound exactly the same as you?

Boy: No.

Jukebox: When several sounds get together, you hear what we call different timbres, or qualities, of sound. Here, let me add a picture of your friend.

Boy: That doesn't look like my friend

Girl: Shhh!

Jukebox: Now sometimes, your friend may want to walk in a different rhythm, or sing in a different place, or even sing a different song from yours. But it can all still be a great sound, and we call that texture. It's like a layer cake of sound. Some layers are different from others, but together it's still a cake.

Girl: Wow, I like your picture of a cake.

Jukebox: One last part to the music. When that cake was baked, the baker couldn't just mix it in the air and throw it into the oven.

Boy: My dad needs a bowl to mix the batter.

Girl: My mom needs a cake pan to bake the cake in the oven.

Jukebox: Well, the bowl or cake pan is like the last part of music we are going to talk about, which is called form. It is the container that gives it meaning or shape.

Boy: I didn't realize music was like going for a walk!

Jukebox: So now you know what is inside of me that allows you to hear music.

Girl: Yeah, you have melody...

Boy: and rhythm...

Girl: timbre...

Boy: texture...

Girl: and form...

Boy: The melody is the hum...

Girl: as we walk to the beat...

Boy: AND talk to the rhythm...

Girl: We use different kinds of sounds to create timbre...

Boy: and different layers to create texture...

Girl: and put it all in some kind of form...

Both: and we have MUSIC.

Girl: I'll never go for another walk.

Boy: Why?

Girl: Too much happening. I'd get too tired to come home!

Jukebox: Well, the magic is almost done for today. Please turn me off now, unplug me, and let me sleep. Come back another day and I will play for you again.

Narrator 1: The children did as the jukebox asked. They crept out of the garage and carefully closed the door.

(Strains of "The Music Goes Round and Round" play as the children file offstage)

✸ Connecting Curriculum: TELLING WHAT WE KNOW ABOUT OUR LEARNING

When students are asked to articulate what they know about their learning, teachers gain valuable insights into their understanding. When students' words are recorded and made into a simple Readers Theatre scripts, children share not only what they know with one another but also with their parents. The script samples on the following pages were developed using the scriptwriting ideas outlined in chapter 5.

"Telling-what-we-know" scripts

Sometimes You Just Know

Reader 1:	Sometimes you just know the words.
Reader 2:	Sometimes you don't.
Reader 1:	That's O.K. There are clues. Yes, there are clues.
Reader 2:	You mean clues like detectives use to figure out a mystery?
Reader 3:	What's a clue for mystery words?
Reader 4:	Sometimes you can look at the pictures and they'll help you figure out the words you don't know.
Reader 5:	I sound the words out.
Reader 2:	Some words don't sound out.
Reader 5:	I break them up and sound out the parts that I can.
Reader 2:	Good detectives use all the information they have to solve mysteries.
Reader 1:	Sure! Skip the mystery word and try to use the pictures and the parts you can read for clues.
Reader 5:	Sometimes I just ask a friend.
Reader 4:	If there's no one to ask I just skip the words I don't know and read the ones I can.
Reader 3:	That makes sense.
Reader 1:	It always makes sense to figure things out.
Reader 2:	I just thought of another way. You can think of another word that is close to the one you're stuck on like *book* and *crook*.
Reader 1:	I bet the kids here could think of more ways, too.
Reader 2:	Let's ask them.

Subtraction

Five young kids sitting at the park...

1: My brother thinks he's SO big just because he gets to do SUBTRACTION! What's subtraction?

2: Well... it means flying away.

1: Flying away?

2: Yeah; like 6 birds in a tree and 2 fly away. THAT'S subtraction.

1: Oh...

3: No! It means eating!

1: Eating?

3: Yeah; you have 4 apples and you eat 1. THAT'S subtraction.

1: Oh...

4: No! It's...

1: My allow...

4: Yeah; you go to the store with 10 cents and you spend 5 cents. THAT'S subtraction.

1: Oh!

5: No! It's taking away!

1: Taking away?

5: Yeah; you have 12 marbles and your brother takes 8. THAT'S subtraction!

1: Oh...subtraction's not so tough. I gotta go now. Bye!

ALL: THAT'S SUBTRACTION!!

Skit   May.15/95

Characters

Narrator
Reader 1
Reader 2
Reader 3
Reader 4

Nar – One of these nice sunny days me and my buds were walking down town.

R1 – have you studied for the test on Monday

R2 – what's studying?

R3 – it's when you look at your nails

Nar – and then she started quizzing us

R1 – do you even know what a ray is?

R3 – isn't ray the new guy that work at the ice cream parlor.

R2 – No a ray is something you shave with.

R1 – No a ray is a stream of light.

Nar – then she asked us the hardest question of all.

R1 – Are any of you smart enough to know what speed light travels at?

R3 – NO what do you think I am smart or something.

R4 – I know the answer to that question.

R2 – Okay what is it then.

R4 – light travels at a speed of 300,000,000 metrs per second.

R3 – Fine then smarty pants.

Nar – Then me and my friends continued on our way

Nar – She ... sma ... wh...

R2 – ...

R3 – Ye...

R4 – No, a ... tog...

All together –

Sources of Light

Nar   F.L
Sun   L.B

Nar. What is light? I never understood it.

Sun. For instance I am a source of light. I am the sun

F.L. Yeah you light up our lives

L.B. Because I produce light, I am luminous

F.L. Talk about luminous.

Nar. I still don't get it! How does light travel

Sun. Light travels in straight lines which are called rays.

Nar. Ohh! I get it!

L.B. I don't produce light sometimes!

Sun. Light Bulbs need electricity to work. Just turn yourself on.

L.B. I can't, I can't turn me on! I'm afraid of the dark.

Nar, Sun, F.L. Click!

Sun, L. B, F.L. Do you get it now?

Nar. Not really. All I know is when a flashlight is on it produces straight lines of light that are called rays. Rays come together and make a beam, which hits an object to make it show, that is called illuminato.

"Telling-what-we-know" scripts

"Readers Theatre"

May. 9 '95

Color

Dumb Student(s)   Student #2 (Stu #2)
Student #1 (Stu#1)   Student #3 (Stu #3)

Stu. #3: He is so stupid!

Stu. #2: You got that right!

Stu. #1: He doesn't even know who Isaac Newton is.

D.S.: I know who he is! He made up Snoopy.

Stu. #3: No, he's the guy who tested his theory and produced beautiful colors through a prism.

Stu. #1: Yeah, and he called it a spectrum!

Stu. #2: But what is a spectrum?

D.S.: I know what it is, it's a speck on a drum.

Stu. #1: No, No, a spectrum is when you have your prism in the path of a light, and you

see beautiful colors.

Stu. #3: Hey guys, what's white light?

D.S.: I know what white light is. It's light that is white.

Stu. #2: No, white light is all of the colors in the spectrum mixed together.

Stu. #1: Did you know that an object is green because it absorbs all of the colors of the spectrum except for green! Then it reflects the green pigment back to the eye.

D.S.: Then why is an object black and and what colors reflect?

Stu. #3: An object is black because it absorbs all of the colors of the spectrum and it reflects no colors.

D.S.: But guys, how do we see light?

boy!

Refraction

May 15. '95

Narrator
Alien 1
Alien 2
Human 1
Human 2

Human 1 - "What's that in the sky!"
Human 2 - "It's a bird, it's a plane."
Human 1 - "It is superman."
Human 2 - "No it's not it's aliens."

Narrator - Down came the space ship and the doors opened. Out came two little aliens.

Human 1 - "Look here they come."

Alien 1+2 - "Hello people from planet Zerk."

Human 2 - "I think you are mistaken, this is planet Earth."

Alien 1 - "Oh, we must of refracted the wrong way."
Alien 2 - "Dense head."

Human 1 - "Those guys aren't normal."
Human 2 - "What is refraction anyway."

Alien 2 - "Refraction is the bending of light as it passes from one medium to another."
Alien 1 - "Well, I guess we better get going, we have a schedual to keep on planet Zerk."

Human 1+2 - "Bye, for now?"

All - The ray the aliens refracted off is called the refracted ray. Some other rays are called the incident ray and the emergent ray.

Reflection

Nar. 1
Nar. 2
Light Beam
Scientist
Bartholomew

Nar 1. - One day this child, Bartholomew, walked into a large science lab.

Nar. 2 - He saw a scientist and asked him some questions

Bartholomew - What is an incident ray?

Scientist - An incident ray is the original ray of light. Here is an example. Watch the beam of light travel to the mirror.

Beam - Watch me!

Scientist - The beam that you see coming off of the mirror is the reflected ray. Blah, Blah, Blah.

Nar. 1. And here we are, twenty minutes later...

Scientist - And understand?

Bartholomew - W

Beam - I am per second. the incident ra

Nar. 2 - Then Bartholomew asked another question.

Bartholomew - What is the ray after it reflects?

Scientist - Lets go back to the beam for the answer.

Beam - After I hit the mirror I became the reflected ray.

Bartholomew - What is the normal line?

Scientist - The normal line is a right angled line between the incident and reflected rays.

Nar. 1. - The inquisitive Bartholomew asks two more questions.

Bartholomew - Well, smarty pants what is the angle of incidence and the angle of reflection.

Scientist - Well the angle of reflection is the angle between the normal line and the reflected ray. And the angle of incidence is the angle between the normal line and the incident ray.

Bartholomew - Oh yeah? Well why is the sea blue and green but not just one color?

✳ *Connecting Curriculum:* READERS THEATRE FOR VERY YOUNG CHILDREN

Using familiar stories, rhymes, and predictable stories, emergent readers can be taught the basics of Readers Theatre. Once children have memorized the words, they are assigned a color that corresponds to the line they have memorized. Then the color-coded parts, rather than the print, are used as markers to assist young readers.

For example, with a poem such as the following, the teacher assigns each reader or group of readers a color. The teacher writes one line each on manila tag strips, using a different color marker for each reader. He or she then holds up the cards in order. Children who have memorized the poem will identify their color and recite their line. This exercise also helps them begin to recognize words.

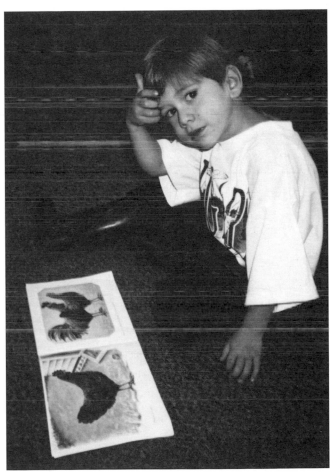

Red:	Old Mother Hubbard
Blue:	Went to the cupboard
Yellow:	To get the poor dog a bone.
Blue:	When she got there
Red:	The cupboard was bare
Yellow:	So the poor dog had none.

Begin with paired reading, one line per reader:

Green:	Humpty Dumpty sat on a wall
Purple:	Humpty Dumpty had a great fall
Green:	All the King's horses
Purple:	And all the King's men
Green:	Couldn't put Humpty together
Purple:	Again!

Build on this by assigning parts to more readers or groups of readers:

Blue: Humpty Dumpty

Red: Sat on a wall

Blue: Humpty Dumpty

Green: Had a great fall

Red: All the King's horses

Blue: And all the King's men

Green: Couldn't put Humpty together

All Readers: Again!

Use skipping rhymes:

Red: My mother said

Green: I never should

Red: Follow bears in the wood

Green: If I did

Red: She would say

Green: Naughty boy/girl to disobey

Red: How many times would she say?

All readers: One, two, three, four…

Purple: Jack and Jill

Green: Went up the hill

Purple: To fetch a pail of water.

Green: Jack fell down

Purple: And broke his crown

Green: And Jill came tumbling after.

Purple: Up Jack got

Green: And home did trot

Purple: As fast as he could caper.

Green: Went to bed

Purple: To mend his head

Green: With vinegar and brown paper.

Predictable books and traditional children's action rhymes are a great source of patterns that are already known by children or can be easily memorized. These activities provide important jumping-off points for beginning readers.

✻ Connecting Curriculum: STUDENTS WRITE THEIR OWN READERS THEATRE SCRIPTS

Students can compose their own Readers Theatre scripts using the structures and procedures outlined in chapter 5. Following are some topics to initiate ideas:

- Describe a person.
- Describe a place.
- Describe a thing.
- Advertise.
- Promote an idea.
- Introduce a concept.
- Show diversity.
- Make a point.

Student-written script

Name: _____ Date: _____

Title: Science 7

Characters: Reflected Ray   Readers: _____
          Incident Ray
          Normal
          Nr. 1
          Nr. 2
          Nr. 3

Reader N1 : Let's reflect on light.

Reader N2 : You mean reflection.

Reader N3 : Ya reflection. What is a ray?

Reader In.R.: Well I am an incident ray.

Reader N1 : What is that?

Reader In.R.: The original light ray.

Reader N2 : What happens when the incident ray hits an object?

Reader N3 : It reflects and makes a reflected ray.

Reader Re.R.: I'm the reflected ray.

Reader In.R.: But there is something in common between us.

Reader N3 : That's not normal.

Reader Nor : Course not, I'm normal. I'm the one.

Reader Re.R : What's that?

Reader In.R.: The angle of incidence and the angle of reflection.

Reader N1 : They have the same angle going in.

Reader N3 : and the angle going out.

Reader All : Okay we understand.

Reader N3 : Let's reflect back on what we have learned.

Many classroom activities, such as journal writing, group meetings, sharing work, and readers clubs, support Readers Theatre. Becoming better in Readers Theatre means becoming better at telling one's own stories. Once you can tell your own stories then you are better able to tell someone else's story.

Readers Theatre practice and invention provides children with opportunities to play with language, ways to demonstrate their knowledge about a topic, and another form for publishing their ideas.

Publishing activities web

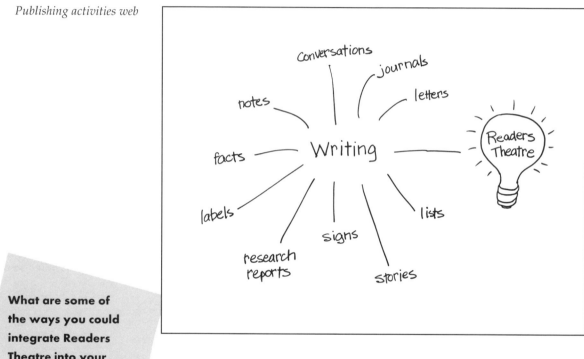

What are some of the ways you could integrate Readers Theatre into your teaching of different curriculum concepts?

EVALUATION

Evaluation is an important companion to instruction. Readers Theatre is enhanced by evaluation that supports student learning. In Readers Theatre, we may choose to evaluate the script, the direction, and the performance, focusing on the features outlined in the evaluation form below.

Teachers, when assisting students to articulate their learning, help children develop self-direction and autonomy. Reflection and self-evaluation help students gain a sense of what they can do and what they can improve upon. In this way, students, by knowing what they value in their own work, become contributors to the evaluation process.

When students are involved in building collections of work—evidence of their own learning—they begin to identify and value their own strengths and to search those areas that need improvement. Collections of work give students, teachers, and parents insight into the learner's growth and development.

When teachers include parents, students, and teachers as valued contributors to reporting, communication is improved. When everyone has a chance to take part, ask for clarification, see

---

Readers Theatre Evaluation Criteria

What makes a good script?

- Is it interesting (containing conflict, imagery, variety, rhyme, pattern, repetition, humor, surprise ending, character appeal)?
- Does the language invoke images for the listening audience?
- Is there balance between readers and narration?
- Does the dialogue flow? Is there a steady pace?
- Is it written for a particular age group? If so, is the material age-appropriate?
- Does it consider the reading abilities of the reader?
- Does it consider the listening abilities of the audience (length of the script, vocabulary)?
- Are clear directions included (directions may change during rehearsals)?
- Does the script remain true to the original text?

What makes a good reader?

- Does he or she use voice effectively (projection, pitch, emphasis, inflection, enunciation, intonation, expression)?
- Is reader familiar with the script and able to read the material?
- Does reader knows his/her place in the script?
- Does reader demonstrate confidence and enthusiasm?
- Does he or she use actions to enhance the presentation (maintaining character role; using body language effectively; handling script without distraction; avoiding upstaging, overacting, mugging and overuse of facial expressions; using offstage focus)?
- Does reader recognize cues?
- Is reader able to pace himself/herself effectively?
- Does reader use props effectively?(Note: the script is a prop)

What makes a good presentation?

- Does the performance appear to be rehearsed (not memorized but practiced)?
- Are any props used. If so, do they enhance performance?
- Are the stage directions effective (back to audience, step forward, head bowed, entering and exiting the stage)?
- How are the readers positioned? Is elevation used? (Note readers stance, use of chairs, stools, benches.)
- Is the audience able to see and hear the cast members?
- Is each reader contributing to the success of the performance? (Note what makes a good reader's voice, actions, and pace.)
- Collectively, is there continuous flow and smooth transitions throughout the performance?

specific examples, and know they've been heard, future learning is understood and supported.

When students set goals based on what they have learned and need to learn, they have a clear direction and support. Teachers and students collaborate to set criteria for these "next steps" to learning.

In this chapter we provide many ideas for self-evaluation and reflection, and for collecting evidence of learning, setting criteria with students, sharing accomplishments with parents, and setting goals for the future. Please adapt them for use with *your* students in *your* classroom.

Evaluation:

What assessment and evaluation strategies already work for you and your children?

✸ *Evaluation:* SPECIFIC COMPLIMENTS

To help your students become specific in their observations, take advantage of their natural ability to respond. Following each presentation, ask presenters to invite compliments. When students begin giving compliments, their responses lack detail; compliments such as "It was good" abound. As students learn to give specific compliments, we ask the person giving the compliment, "What made it good?" Children then respond with more detail.

For example:

Teacher:	What did you like about the performance?
Student:	It was good.
Teacher:	What made it good?
Student 1:	I really liked the way your voice changed.
Student 2:	I really liked the way you held your paper so we could hear your voice and see your face.
Student 3:	I really liked the way you helped Susan. It was hard to tell there was a problem.

Compliments become a way of life in the classroom. As students and teachers generate lists of what makes Readers Theatre scripts and presentations effective, they not only develop ideas for compliments but also come to understand and appreciate the elements of effective Readers Theatre. Students are then ready to use these as criteria for assessment and evaluation.

✸ *Evaluation:* COLLABORATIVE CRITERIA SETTING

When children are involved in outlining the characteristics of a successful project, they learn what to aspire to and what they already do well. This information provides them with direction for goal setting and the knowledge they need to guide their work on a daily basis.

To generate this information, ask students, "What makes a Readers Theatre performance successful?" Record their responses. Use the following sample questions to help students become more specific:

Questions about the performers

- What will be seen when people are reading well?
- What makes the reading interesting? (For example, clarity, projection, variety of voice, expression, enunciation, focus, sensitivity)
- What is it important to remember when we're reading?
- How do we need to be sitting (standing, kneeling, squatting)?
- What will the listeners be doing?
- What do you want others to notice about your reading?

Questions about the script

- What makes the script interesting? entertaining? good to listen to?
- What is a good balance between the narrators and the characters?
- Is the blocking design effective? What makes it effective? What could make it more effective?
- Are the readers comfortable with the script? Does it read well?
- Does the script have a clear beginning, middle and end?
- Does the script work?

Questions about the audience

- What will we see in the audience's reaction?
- Do you hold the attention of the audience?
- Does the audience sit quietly and keep eyes on the readers?
- Are audience members able to tell about the important parts of the story?

Questions about presentation

- How will we know if we have done a good job?

Ask students to work with one or two other people and develop a personal checklist that includes the elements of an effective Readers Theatre script and performance. Students can use this checklist to assess and evaluate their own work and the work of their classmates. The lists on the following pages are the result of collaboration between students and teacher. They are used by students for self-assessment and by the teacher for evaluation.

What makes a good script?

- Is it interesting? (conflict, imagery, variety, rhyme, pattern, repetition, humor, surprise, ending, character appeal.)
- Does the language invoke images for the listening audience?
- Is there balance between readers and narration?
- Does the dialog flow? Is there a steady pace?
- Is it written for a particular age group? If so, is the material age-appropriate?
- Does it consider the reading abilities of the reader?
- Does it consider the listening abilities of the audience? (length of script, vocabulary)
- Are clear directions included?
- Does the script remain true to the original text?

Student/teacher-generated checklists

What makes a good reader?

- Effective use of voice (projection, pitch, emphasis, inflection, enunciation, intonation, expression)
- Familiar with the script and able to read the material
- Knows his/her place in the script.
- Demonstrates confidence and shows enthusiasm
- Actions used enhance the presentation (maintains character role, effective use of body language, handles script without distraction, avoids upstaging, over-acting, mugging (over use of facial expressions), use of off stage focus)
- Recognizes cues and is able to pace him/herself effectively
- Use of props (note: the script is a prop)

What makes a good presentation?

- Does the performance appear to be rehearsed? (not memorized, but practiced)
- Are any props used? If so, do they enhance performance?
- Are the stage directions used effectively? (back to audience, step forward, head bowed, entering and exiting the stage)
- How are the readers positioned? Is elevation used? (readers stance, use of chairs, stools, benches)
- Is the audience able to see and hear the cast members?
- Is each reader contributing to the success of the performance? (note what makes a good reader's voice, actions, and pace)
- Collectively, are there continuous flow and smooth transitions throughout the performance?

Name Isabelle Black   **Date** May 12   **Class** 14

What I want you to notice: that my script is finished

Criteria	✔	Student Observation/Comment
1. remains true to original text		it's the same as the fairy tale
2. balance of readers and narrators		I counted lines and they are just about equal.
3. interesting story		I like this fairy tale and so does my little buddy.
4. language invokes images for audience		I've used powerful words like red hot, gowling, scampered

You should know: that I worked really hard to balance the readers and narrators. I hope our buddies like the performance.

Reproducible master in Appendix A

Name _____   **Date** _____

The Readers Theatre I've written called _____ is attached.

An effective Readers Theatre script/performance has the following characteristics:

Characteristics	Evidence (Proof)
☐ everyone says about the same amount	they do - see script
☐ the audience can see everyone's face (blocking)	they can - see blocking
☐ the story is interesting	the class really listened and laughed at the funny parts.
☐ the words help make pictures in your mind	they said that the old man was a real grump and that means they forgot it was Matthew
☐ the story has a beginning, a middle, and an end	It does and I put a * at the places in the script

✿ *Evaluation:* STUDENT SELF-ASSESSMENT

When teachers help students describe their learning, students develop self-direction and autonomy. Reflection and self-evaluation help them gain a sense of what they can do and what they can improve upon. In this way, students, by knowing what they value in their own work, become contributors to the evaluation process.

By using the questions found on pages 69–70 or the evaluation characteristics found on page 67, more open-ended frames can be developed. Sometimes all students use the same frame; at other times students use those of their own design. The guiding principle is that the frames focus students' attention on their learning.

Self-assessment frames

Name _____ Date _____

Today we _____

The part I enjoy the most is _____

The part I am best at is _____

The part I most want to improve in is _____

Next time I'd like to _____

Name _____ Date _____

The language in my script is powerful because _____

There is a balance between narration and dialogue. I can prove this by _____

The dialogue has a good pace. I know this because _____

This script is written for a _____ reader. I know that this kind of reader can read this script. My proof is _____

The directions are clear. For example _____

This script could be improved by _____

Next time I write a script I will _____

Name _____ Date _____

Three things I know about my character are _____

My character begins feeling _____
and ends feeling _____

My character's role can be described by the following words:
_____

Name _____ Date _____

I have been practicing my reading of the script called _____

I have been practicing with _____

I read this script _____
I know this because _____

I use body language when _____

I use vocal coloring when _____

I could improve my script reading by _____

Next time I am read a script I will _____

✱ *Evaluation:* STUDENT SELF-ASSESSMENT VIDEOS

Performance videos are powerful evaluation tools. They can be used in many ways:

- ☞ Ask students to select the attribute they need to watch for (for example, use of vocal coloring) and then ask them to reflect on their findings in a journal.
- ☞ Give students a form with space for two compliments and a wish. Ask them to watch the performance and fill out the form for themselves or for the entire performance group.
- ☞ Ask students to select criteria for an excellent performance, then analyze their own performances using that criteria.

Video evaluation forms

Name _____ Date _____

I'm focusing on the following criteria for an effective Readers Theatre perform[...]

_____   _____
_____   _____
_____   _____

I know I have improved/met the criteria because when you watch the video of m[...] you'll notice

1. _____
   _____
   _____

2. _____
   _____
   _____

3. _____
   _____
   _____

Parent Comment

Dear _____ ,

We just want you to know that _____
and next time please _____

Name : _____ Date: _____

Character's Name: _____

Performance Attributes	Comment Evidence
Character { Voice of character (vocal coloring) / Clarity of voice / Movement / Staging in character / Props / clothing	
Staging { Blocking - changes/not static / Everyone visible (no masking of other performers)	
Presentation { Flows / Clearly understandable / Enjoyable	

✷ *Evaluation:* GROUP SELF-REPORTING FRAMES

When teachers help student groups think about their work together, they develop self-direction and autonomy. Reflection and self-evaluation help groups gain a sense of what they can do and what they can improve upon. When all students work together and learn to function as an effective group, each student benefits as a group member. Student groups can be guided to work effectively when teachers structure experiences so everyone has a meaningful role within that group.

Group self-reporting frame

Group Self-Report

Members _____ Date _____

_____

Task _____

The best part of working together was _____
_____
_____
_____

The part we need to improve the most is _____
_____
_____
_____

One problem we had was _____
_____
_____
_____

We solved it by _____
_____
_____
_____

signed _____
_____

✹ *Evaluation:* RATING SCALES

Once we have set criteria with our students, it is easy to develop rating scales for our groups. Whether your students are involved in storytelling, scriptwriting, or performing, rating scales help students assess themselves and provide evidence of learning to teachers. Three sample

Rating forms rating scales are illustrated.

Volume	inaudible	├─┼─┼─┼─┤	audible
Clarity	mumbled	├─┼─┼─┼─┤	clear
Eye contact	not appropriate	├─┼─┼─┼─┤	appropriate
Stance	poor posture	├─┼─┼─┼─┤	good posture
Mannerisms	detract from character	├─┼─┼─┼─┤	enhance character
Intonation	monotone	├─┼─┼─┼─┤	varied and appropriate

Adapted from *Oral Communication in the Classroom,* B.C. Ministry of Education Document XX0101, January 1988.

Name _____ **Date** _____ **to** _____

Group Members
_____

Rating Criteria
1. Rarely observed
2. Sometimes observed
3. Frequently observed
(becoming characteristic of students)

Readers Theatre Presentation of *Wizard of Oz*	Group Self-Rating 1 2 3	Comments Student	Teacher
1. Script rehearsed	☐ ☐ ✔	We practiced 12 times	
2. Props add to performance	☐ ✔ ☐	The hats really worked!	
3. Stage directions are used effectively	☐ ✔ ☐	We kept getting our turns wrong	
4. Blocking adds to success of performance	☐ ☐ ✔	Thanks for helping with this!	
5. Audience able to see and hear cast members	☐ ☐ ✔	It worked!	
6. Readers have appropriate voice, actions, pace	☐ ✔ ☐	We're getting better. The Tinman's voice was outstanding because it carried to the back and had great coloring	
7. Smooth transitions throughout performance	✔ ☐ ☐	There weren't many changes for this script	
Summary Comments			

Name *Chris Stewart* **Date** *April*

Script title *The Dirtbike Racer*

Rating
Yes, I'm doing well
No, I need to improve

Criteria for *Reading a Readers Theatre Script*	Rating scale yes/no	Self-Evaluation Comment on your script reading	Ask someone else to comment on your script reading
effective use of voice (volume, articulation, vocal coloring)	Y?	I think I've gotten better. Joe said he could hear me from the back.	I heard him at the back.
familiar with script and able to read material	Y	I practiced it. I helped write it so I know how it goes	He sounded good and he didn't get mixed up.
knows place in script	Y	I highlighted my lines so I'm ready.	Seemed right to me.
recognizes cues and paces reading	Y	I'm not bad — I only missed one cue.	Good. I didn't know he missed one.
Uses props (script) effectively	Y	I wore my helmet, shinpads, and chest protector.	They all looked great.
Shows confidence, commitment, and willingness to try	? Y	I like doing this for our buddies.	He's good at this. Joe H.
I am pleased because *the buddies clapped when we were finished.*			
My next steps for improving are *Learning how to write exciting scripts.*			

Reproducible masters in Appendix A

Evaluation: STORY COLLECTOR'S RECORD

When students collect evidence of their own learning—work samples, checklists, completed criteria—they begin to identify and value their own strengths and acknowledge those areas that need improvement. These collections of work give students, teachers, and parents more insight into the learner's growth and development.

The following frames help students record their experiences with storytelling, scriptwriting, and Readers Theatre performances.

Record forms

Personal Storytelling Record   Name _____

Story Name	Content	Where I found it	Who I told it to	When I told it
Hansel + Gretel	fairytale	home	some grade ones in the library	Nov. 16
The Lie	story from my Dad	home	my friends	December
When I was Young in the Artic	about when I lived in Inuvik	it's about me	my Priend's mom	December

Readers Theatre Participation Record

Name ___Ramona Louis___   Date ___January___

Readers theatre title ___The Princess and The Pea___

My part ___The Princess___

My group members ___Joe, Mary, Jordan___

Director ___Ms. Drake___

Comment ___We performed this for a sharing assembly___

Each classroom teacher has a different emphasis depending upon the needs, interests, age, and ability of her students. Checklists are helpful for collecting a wide range of information. One teacher reviewed her curriculum and her students' needs and interests, developed a list of potential ideas, and selected a focus for one term. The focus became the basis for her Readers Theatre checklist.

Web and observation checklist

Observation Checklist Readers Theatre (primary)	Isabelle	Susan	Chris	Lisa	Ross	Marta	Huan	Luisa	Dan	Kim	Leah	Carmen	Raj	Maria	Toaa
loves to play with sounds of language															
understands the story															
open to ideas expressed by others															
varies voice tone when reading															
varies speed (tempo) of voice when reading															
interprets the characters															
chooses performing center frequently															
articulates words															
eager to have a part															
writes scripts:															
writes one word															
writes conversation															
adapts stories															
adapts books															
loves to write															
loves to read															
seeks out ideas															

loves to play with the sounds of language

writes scripts
- simple one word
- conversation
- story
- published story

enthusiasm
- for writing
- for reading

understands the story/text itself

seeks out new ideas/materials

open to ideas expressed by others

Readers Theatre (developing skills)

eager to have a part

Contributes ideas for
- staging
- script
- performance

varies voice
- tone
- tempo

articulates words

reads parts smoothly/easily

chooses performing center frequently

interprets the character

✹ *Evaluation:* USING JOURNALS

Students can keep journals as an ongoing record of their thinking and work in Readers Theatre. Because their work leaves no visible trace, recording insights gained through practice and interaction with classmates solidifies students' learning and provides a record for later evaluation.

It helps to provide students with an open-ended starting point. Sometimes a teacher will be tempted to direct part of the journal entry; resist this urge, or students will cease to feel ownership for the journal and its effectiveness will disappear.

Student reflections

JUN 14 1994

I like readers theatre because we have to read scrips. I like readers theatre because it is challenging. I like readers theatre because we don't have to memo I like readers theatre because We have to practice. I like being Nicodemus in readers theatre because I like how I did my wice I like Nicodemus because he is old wise and smart.

Readers Theatre

I like readers theatre because we don't have to memorize our scipts. I like the way that other people do their voices. I like to listen to the people that do the play. I like the way the people change voices. I like to do plays because I li to read to oth people. I like the that people that soft voices chang to high voices.

June 14   1994

① I like readers Theatre because I like to change my voice and to watch people do it to. ② I like how other people can change voices. ③ When people do reade theatre they have to have voices loud enough so that ever body who is listening to you can hear you. ④ Reader theatre is fun. ⑤ Some peop hate to do readers theatre and just want to watch. ⑥ I like to do readers theatre when I have re the book or seen er is th eak in

---

JUN 14 1994 Readers Theatre

I like Readers theatre when I get lots of lines beacause I like being almost the main character in that chapter. And I like to practice my voice. I like to speak clearly. And I some like working with bossy people. I like having challenging words. And I like memorizing the senteces. And I would like to be the Narrator.

Very good thoughts

June 14, 94   Readers Theatre (1-6)

① I like doing Readers Theatre because I get to be a diffrent person.
② I like to be Mrs. Frisby because she's a main character.
③ I really enjoy doing Readers Theatre because I really feel good about getting complaments from every body
④ It's really intresting how every body gets to do different scens because you get to hear diffrent parts
⑤ I really like how every person gets to do a diffrent voice and how you get to change characters every time.
⑥ I get really embarsed when I do a mistake or when I goof up on a word

---

Readers Theatre

June 14, 94

I like Readers Theatre because you get to changing your voices and do lots of lines. I like it because you don't half to memorize the lines and I like it because they go normal reading instead of fast and really slow. And I like it how you change your voices like Mr. Ages and Mrs. Frisby. And how they do pitch high squeaky little voices. And low and bigger and older. And the Narrator does clearly nice voices and loudly.

✲ *Evaluation:* AUDIOTAPING

The tape recorder is an effective tool that offers students a way to observe their growing power over language, both spoken and written. Possibilities for using audiotapes are numerous—two are detailed below.

1. Record students efforts with expressive language three times over the year to document the progress they have made. Sample reading materials could include

   - a sentence read with different tempos
   - a sentence read with different kinds of vocal coloring
   - a student-written script

2. Have students record and analyze an audiotape of a script rehearsal. Progressive rehearsals can be collected, dated, and later used to compare individual and class growth. Use a variety of criteria appropriate for the age and development of the students.

✲ *Evaluation:* SETTING CHALLENGES FOR FINDING EVIDENCE

One teacher regularly challenges her students to show evidence of their learning. As a summary at the end of a Readers Theatre experience, students are asked to tell about, write about or show evidence of some of the following:

Student statements

> I learned that it is scary to stand in front of everyone. Next time I'm going to use a music stand.

> I was surprised that our parents like the sharing assembly. They said that I made my voice sound really, really mad and they could hear that.

> I was surprised that the primaries really wanted to ask us questions. They asked good questions. I think we should do the Peacekeepers Readers Theatre again.

> I didn't want to work with Georgia because I thought she didn't like me. We used Uncle Al's formula and it turned out great. We did a good job when we read Cinderella to Ms. Fraser's class.

- something they have learned
- something they are proud of
- solving a problem
- something they did with someone else
- something they found hard to do
- a mistake they realized they had made
- something that their teacher would be surprised they could do
- something they were surprised they could do
- something they wanted to have more time to do

9

INVITING, INCLUDING, AND INFORMING OTHERS

When we invite, include, and inform others—our parents, administrators, colleagues and school community—we gain support and enrich our practice.

What parents hear from their children or what they see them doing at school may seem very different from their own recollections as students. Parents who are included, invited, and informed are more likely to develop an understanding of why you are using Readers Theatre and be supportive of what is taking place in the classroom.

Like us, school administrators are busy people with specific jobs to accomplish. The best way to rally their support for what is happening in our classrooms is to include, invite, and inform them. This can be accomplished by

- talking to them about what you are doing
- inviting them to your classroom to watch your students preparing and performing Readers Theatre scripts
- ensuring every letter that goes home to parents also goes to them
- recognizing their expertise and asking them to act as resource people
- involving them in the process as a possible audience

What do you do that helps your parent community feel comfortable about your classroom?

This chapter contains a number of ways to invite, include, and inform others. Please adapt them to suit the needs of yourself, your students, and your school community.

Inviting, Including and Informing Others:

Inviting, Including, and Informing Others: SUBJECT NIGHTS

We invite parents to hear about details of our classroom program while watching their children shine as performers. On this evening, every child needs a chance to be heard and seen. Using Readers Theatre scripts written by children to describe math, gym, or any aspect of their day in school, entertains parents while informing them. All sessions follow a similar format:

1. Children and parents arrive to tour the classroom.
2. Parents watch children performing and informing.
3. Teacher is available for questions and/or comments.
4. Everyone shares refreshments (optional) and says good night.

To prepare,

- children and teacher prepare a Readers Theatre script which highlights, for example, a specific curriculum area or the elements of the students timetable
- children practice their parts and finalize its presentation (in terms of placement of readers and use of any props)
- children write an invitation to their parents, asking them to bring a small snack to share and enough juice for their family members
- teacher posts an agenda where it can be easily seen; a parent response form is designed and copied

Parent Night agenda and script

Agenda	Time 6:30 – 7:30 pm.
Welcome	
Tour the classroom	
News Broadcast performance by Div. 12	
Refreshments	
Goodnight	

Parent Night

Division ____

Roles for Readers	Student's name
Anchorperson 1 (AP1)	
Anchorperson 2 (AP2)	
On-site reporter 1 (R1	
On-site reporter 2 (R2	
On-site reporter 3 (R3	
On-site reporter 4 (R4	
On-site reporter 5 (R5	
On-site reporter 6 (R6	
On-site reporter 7 (R7	
Interviewee 1 (I1)	
Interviewee 2 (I2)	
Interviewee 3 (I3)	
Interviewee 4 (I4)	
Interviewee 5 (I5)	
Interviewee 6 (I6)	
Interviewee 7 (I7)	
Advertiser 1 (A1)	
Advertiser 2 (A2)	
Advertiser 3 (A3)	
Advertiser 4 (A4)	
Advertiser 5 (A5)	
Advertiser 6 (A6)	
Advertiser 7 (A7)	
Advertiser 8 (A8)	

To stage the following perimeter of the room. returns to them after e

Anchorperson 1: Good evening, listeners, I'm _____ [AP1].

Anchorperson 2: And I'm _____ [AP2].

Anchorperson 1: This is the evening news program from (*school initials and division number, e.g., MB12*).

Anchorperson 2: brought to you live from _____ (*name of school and division number, e.g., Miracle Beach School, Division 12*)

Anchorperson 1: Tonight we are going to introduce you to the program in which the _____ (grade) students will be involved this year. The teachers explained to us that all the different aspects of learning school are interwoven and connected. For these purposes, we're taking them apart to show you.

Anchorperson 2: To help you understand this we have on-site reporters who will give us an in-depth focus on different aspects of life in the classroom. Now over to _____ [R1], who is one of our language arts reporters. Come in, _____ [R1].

Reporter 1: Thank you, _____ [AP2] I have some interesting news about the writing section of the language arts program. One of the students is standing by to tell you about this. _____ [I1], what are the types of tasks you will be participating in this year?

Interviewee 1: (*Description of the writing program inserted here*)

Reporter 1: Thanks, _____ [I1]. As you can see, the students will be truly challenged with the writing tasks this year. This is _____ [R1] reporting from writing.

Anchorperson 1: Thank you, _____ [R1]. Our other language arts reporter is _____ [R2]. What have you got for us, _____ [R2]?

Reporter 2: Hi, _____ [AP1]. We have lots of information about reading. I have just been speaking to a number of students about the reading activities for this year, and here is _____ [I2] to summarize what they have told me.

Interviewee 2: (*Description of reading program inserted here.*)

Reporter 2: Great! Thanks, _____ [I2], that was most interesting, and of course best of luck for the year from all of us. That's all we have from here. _____ [R2] reporting.

Anchorperson 2: Thank you, _____ [R2]. More news after this brief break.

Advertiser 1: Say, what do you have for lunch at school each Friday?

Reproducible master in Appendix B

✿ Inviting, Including, and Informing Others: SHARING ASSEMBLIES

Many school communities are finding the organization of a full concert production difficult, if not impossible, given our crowded days. One teaching staff decided to forego concerts and introduce "sharing assemblies" to allow students to "show what they know" to a larger audience.

Different classes decide what part of their classroom learning activities they would like to show. Some prepare a special performance, others bring samples of work such as dioramas, while others teach a playground game or give a skipping demonstration.

Sharing assembly agenda and script

Dates are set early in the year, the gym is booked, and parents are invited. With a teacher's guidance, children act as masters of ceremonies. It is an opportunity for children to show leadership in learning.

One teacher took the idea of the sharing assembly and combined it with Readers Theatre. His entire class of grade-three students acted as masters of ceremonies. The teacher and his class prepared a Readers Theatre script that joined the events of the assembly into a whole, introduced the students and classes presenting, and informed the audience.

Sharing Assembly
Agenda

Welcome! (Principal)

Ms. Sandland & Ms. Krainer's Class
Ms. Mahabir's Class
The Grade Two Students
The Kindergarten Students
Mrs. Hurford's Class
Mrs. Thran's Class
All the Grade One Students
Mrs. Isenor's Class
Choir

Conclusion

Thanks to Brian Goodwin and his grade 3 students.

Spring Concert Script /95
Radical Riddles

Scene 1

Announcer: Welcome boys and girls, teachers and parents to the Radical Riddles Game Show. This promises to be a fast paced, action packed 1/2 hour of riddles and answers. A riddle will be asked and the first contestant who answers it correctly will get points. And the contestant who has the most points at the end of the game wins a beautiful prize.
Let's now give a warm welcome to the host and hostess of our fabulous show Mr. Ricky Riddler and Yanna.

Ricky Riddler: Thank you J.J. for that beautiful introduction. Yanna, you look lovely as usual. Let's get straight to our game and introduce our three contestants. First we have our school teacher from the Insane Asylum. Please welcome Mr. Frank Frazzled. Next we have an ambulance driver. Please welcome Mrs Sally Stitches. Our third contestant today is a principal of an elementary school. Please welcome Mr. Gary Grumpy.
Good luck contestants and let's get started. Here's riddle #1 - What is round, alive, and colourful?

Sally   Mr. Goodwin after he has eaten a big dinner and he's wearing his pink bathing suit?

R. Riddler   Sorry Sally. Nice try.

Frank   A polka dotted whale?

R. Riddler   I'm sorry, that is not the correct answer.

Gary   Give Gary 100 points when Ricky starts talking
Is it Mrs. Sandland's and Krainer's class doing a ribbon dance to the Circle of Life?

R. Riddler   Yes, yes you win 100 points. Well done Mr. Grumpy. Now let's watch them perform.

                    (Sandland/Krainer perform)

Scene 11

R. Riddler   Wonderful, WONDERFUL. Now on to our next riddle. Here goes: What's green, speckled and eats bugs?

Sally   A dog in dress-up clothes playing in a barn?

R. Riddler   I'm sorry, thanks for trying.

Frank   Mr. Sanky and Mr. Nash on a coffee break in the fields?

R. Riddler   Yes, I've seen them, but I'm sorry that's not the right answer.

Gary   Give Gary 100 points when Ricky starts talking
Is it Ms. Mahabir's class singing a song called My Little Pony Needs New Shoes?

R. Riddler   Absolutely right Mr. Grumpy! Now let's be quiet and listen to them sing

                    (Ms. Mahabir's class performs)

Scene V

J.J.   Play with hair
Ricky? Yanna? Do you need your hair combed?

R. Riddler   (shakes head) Let's continue with our game. Ready contestants? What is cute and cuddly and always comes back?

Gary   A lost teddy bear?

R. Riddler   I'm sorry, not quite right.

Frank   A rat who has found a home under your bed?

R. Riddler   Oh no, how awful and totally wrong.

Sally   Sally 100 points
Is it the Grade twos singing a song called The Cat Came Back?

R. Riddler   Yes, absolutely correct! Now let's listen.

                    (the grade two's perform)

Scene VI

R. Riddler   What entertainment this show has! How do we afford it? Anyway, on with the show. Our next riddle is: What makes funny movements and looks like a chicken?

Sometimes students of an entire school need to be informed about school news or initiatives. Announcements and newsletters have their place, but Readers Theatre, which informs while it entertains, is often a more effective method.

For example, one school had undertaken a peer mediator project on the playground. Student peacekeepers were trained in peer mediation to help solve playground problems among students. To introduce themselves and their responsibilities to the other students in the school, their teacher helped them write a Readers Theatre script.

The peacekeepers wrote over four thirty-minute periods. The teacher then took their words and ideas away and drafted a script.

Peacekeeper script

The script was presented to students, who added their suggestions, and the teacher redrafted it. The final script was then presented at a whole-school assembly.

Once they completed their presentation, the peacekeepers visited individual classes to answer students' questions.

Peacekeepers

written by Anne Davies in collaboration with
Heather Ferraby, Darry Oudendag and the Tsolum Peacekeepers.

Roles for Readers   **Student Names**

Reader 1 (R1)
Reader 2 (R2)
Reader 3 (R3)
Reader 4 (R4)
Reader 5 (R5)
Reader 6 (R6)
Reader 7 (R7)
Reader 8 (R8)
Reader 9 (R9)
Reader 10 (R10)
Reader 11 (R11)
Reader 12 (R12)
Reader 13 (R13)
Reader 14 (R14)
Reader 15 (R15)
Reader 16 (R16)
Reader 17 (R17)
Reader 18 (R18)
Reader 19 (R19)
Reader 20 (R20)
Reader 21 (R21)
Reader 22 (R22)
Fighter 1 (F1)
Fighter 2 (F2)
Fighter 3 (F3)
Fighter 4 (F4)
Fighter 5 (F5)
Peacekeeper 1 (P1)
Peacekeeper 2 (P2)
Peacekeeper 3 (P3)
Peacekeeper 4 (P4)

Suggested Staging

Audience

*All readers face the audience. F1, F2, F3, F4 s[...]
audience. Peacekeepers wear jackets and fighters wear hats.*

Reader 14:	We listen.
Reader 15:	We are there.
Reader 17:	We like to chat.
Reader 19:	We are interested
Reader 20:	in what you have to say.
Reader 14:	We pay attention.
Reader 16:	We wear big,
Reader 17:	bright,
Reader 18:	red jackets,
Reader 19:	with a fish
Reader 20:	on a big T.
Reader 21:	We are trained to help you solve your pr[...]
Reader 22:	We won't walk away
Reader 21:	when you are talking to us.
Reader 23:	We won't walk away
Reader 21:	from a problem.

Reader 22:	We won't allow
Reader 21:	name calling,
Reader 23:	put-downs,
Reader 24:	or yelling.
Reader 21:	We won't walk away
Reader 22:	without your problem being solved.
Reader 1:	We are helpers,
Reader 3:	not police officers.
Reader 2:	A peacekeeper's job is to help
Reader 4:	students
Reader 5:	think of peaceful ways
Reader 6:	to solve their problems
Reader 4:	by themselves. We do *not* take sides.
Reader 5:	We listen to each of you.
Reader 8:	We try to be calm,
Reader 9:	patient,
Reader 7:	and friendly.
Reader 8:	We assist you
Reader 9:	to solve problems
Reader 10:	between yourselves and others.
Reader 11:	Some of the problems
Reader 12:	we help
Reader 13:	you solve are
Reader 11:	name-calling
Reader 12:	arguing,
Reader 13:	bullying,
Reader 12:	throwing things,
Reader 11:	using foul language,
Reader 13:	pushing,
Reader 11:	stealing,
Reader 12:	physical fights,

Reproducible master in Appendix B

✿ Inviting, Including, and Informing Others: TAKING THE SHOW ON THE ROAD

Sometimes students enjoy a Readers Theatre activity so much and present it so enthusiastically that it is obvious they need more audiences for their performance. Audiences come in many forms —parents, older or younger buddies, grandparents, the seniors in the community, school-board trustees, or students at another school.

Performing for others can be a positive experience. Readers Theatre, because all the readers support each other, is a relatively risk-free way of performing. It introduces students to the pleasures of receiving recognition and applause, yet individuals don't carry the responsibility for a successful performance alone.

Following are some suggestions for finding new audiences:

- ☞ Post a sign in the staff room describing the performances and asking teachers to sign up for available performance times.
- ☞ Put the performance on the agenda for a sharing assembly.
- ☞ Call a nearby seniors' home or hospital and ask whether they would like to offer their residents a performance by children (perhaps followed by a book sharing with the residents).
- ☞ Call the school-board offices and ask if the board members would like a short performance prior to one of their up-coming meetings.

Sign-up sheet for staff room

Readers Theatre Presentations

Room __3__ has __4__ Readers Theatre performances for presentation in individual classrooms.

They are	The Secret Garden	length	10 mins.
	Little Women		10 mins.
	Treasure Island		10 mins.
	Heidi		10 mins.

If you would like to have one or more presented in your room please fill in the details.

Room	Presentation Title	Length	Preferred date & time
6	all of them	40 min.	after recess, Monday 8th a.m.
10	Heidi	10 min	after lunch, Wed. 10th

❖ *Inviting, Including, and Informing Others:* NEWSLETTERS

Newsletter featuring Readers Theatre

Parents appreciate—and sometimes even ask for—newsletters because they keep them informed about what their child is doing at school. Miniature Readers Theatre scripts, sent home for families to practice and perform for themselves with an explanation of their educational benefits, informs parents while providing them with a positive family interaction.

NEWSLETTER

Dear Parent(s):

During the past month we have been using Readers Theatre as a strategy to help students become better readers and better communicators. The script that follows will explain the basics of Readers Theatre and show how Readers Theatre is used in the classroom.

In the school setting, Rea[...]
It is an excellent reading [...]
and their feelings. It can [...]
or concepts. It is a versat[...]
theme or take a story the[...]
by their classmates.

Readers Theatre encour[...]
tone and pitch, and fluen[...]
purposes. This may invol[...]
risers, sitting on stools or [...]
the corner of the classro[...]
songs, letters, plays, and [...]
Theatre.

Readers Theatre is a sim[...]
ready! Your child will or[...]
first Readers Theatre per[...]

Sincerely,

Readers Theatre Goes Home

Roles for Readers	Names
Parent 1/Narrator 1	_____
Parent 2/Narrator 2	_____
Child 1/Mother Bear	_____
Child 2/Father Bear	_____
Child 3/Baby Bear and Goldilocks	_____

Child 1:	We did Readers Theatre today
Parent 1:	What's Readers Theatre?
Child 2:	It's reading a story
Child 2:	in parts.
Parent 1:	What do you mean in parts?
Child 1:	We could be characters
Child 3:	or narrators,
Child 2:	acting with our voices.
Parent 1:	How do you act with your voice?
Child 2:	We have to understand the character...
Child 3:	how the character feels,
Child 2:	thinks,
Child 1:	and acts.
Parent 1:	So you read clearly
Child 3:	and with good expression
Parent 2:	as though you really are the character
Parent 1:	and are acting the way that character feels.
Parent 2:	Do you have a story to show how Readers Theatre works?
Child 2:	Yes, we have a fairy tale we adapted for Readers Theatre
Child 1:	Dad, you read the part of Narrator 2
Child 3:	and Mom you read Narrator 1.
Child 1:	I'll read Father Bear.
Child 2:	I'll be Mother Bear,
Child 3:	while I read the part of Baby Bear and Goldilocks.
Narrator 1:	Once upon a time there were three bears.
Narrator 2:	There was a father, mother, and a baby.
Narrator 1:	They lived in a little house in the woods.
Narrator 2:	One morning, after Mother Bear had made the breakfast
Mother Bear:	Let's go for a walk while the porridge cools.
Father Bear:	Yes, we can enjoy the morning by walking in the woods,
Narrator 1:	said Father Bear.
Narrator 2:	They left the house.
Baby Bear:	It's nice out walking today.

Narrator 1:	While they were out a little girl with golden hair wandered by their house.
Narrator 2:	She could smell the breakfast and decided to go inside.
Narrator 1:	She saw the porridge.
Goldilocks:	I think I'll try some of that,
Narrator 2:	said Goldilocks.
Narrator 1:	She tried the first bowl.
Goldilocks:	Oh, too hot!
Narrator 2:	she exclaimed and tried the second bowl.
Narrator 1:	She tried the third.
Goldilocks:	Just right! I'll eat it all!
Narrator 2:	After that she wandered around the house looking at everything.
Narrator 1:	Then she sat in Father Bear's big chair.
Goldilocks:	Too hard and uncomfortable. I'll try this middle-sized chair.
Narrator 2:	She sat down.
Goldilocks:	Too soft!
Narrator 1:	Then she sat on the smallest chair.
Goldilocks:	Just right! So comfortable. Oops!
Narrator 2:	As she sat down, one of the legs broke off the chair.
Narrator 1:	Goldilocks got up and went into the bedroom.
Narrator 2:	She lay down on Father Bear's bed.
Goldilocks:	Too lumpy and hard.
Narrator 1:	She tried Mother Bear's bed.
Goldilocks:	Too soft.
Narrator 2:	She tried Baby bear's bed.
Goldilocks:	Just right...so-o-o comfortable.
Narrator 1:	and she fell asleep.
Narrator 2:	When the bears arrived back they could tell someone had been in their home.
Father Bear:	Who's been eating my porridge?
Narrator 1:	growled Father Bear.
Mother Bear:	Who's been eating my porridge?

Narrator 1:	she screamed, and ran out of the house.
Narrator 2:	The bears looked at her running off.
Mother Bear:	We won't bother to chase after her.
Baby Bear:	She looked so scared I'm sure she learned a lesson.
Father Bear:	Let's go and eat breakfast. Mother Bear, will you make some more porridge? *(Mother Bear nods)*
Narrator 2:	Father Bear helped Baby Bear repair his chair and Goldilocks never again went into a house without being invited.

Criteria for Effective Readers Theatre

In our classroom this term our skills emphasis has been on being a "good reader" as we perform Readers Theatre. Other times during the year we may focus on scriptwriting or presenting Readers Theatre. Each area of Readers Theatre develops different skills.

What makes a good reader in Readers Theatre?

- Uses voice effectively (projection, pitch, emphasis, inflection, enunciation, intonation, expression)
- Familiar with the script/able to read the material
- Knows his/her own place in the script
- Demonstrates confidence and enthusiasm
- Uses actions to enhance the presentation
- Recognizes cues and can pace him/herself effectively

- -

Readers Theatre: Thinking About My Learning

Name: _____

Date: _____

I am improving as a reader in Readers Theatre. I know this because:

In order to improve even more I need to:

What do you think?

How could you find out what parents and others really want to know?

Inviting, Including, and Informing Others: SHARING THE LEARNING WITH PARENTS

If we begin a study of Readers Theatre by having children record what they know about it, we prepare ourselves to effectively share what children have learned. The students read over their list of what they knew before beginning work on Readers Theatre and comment on what they know now. When they apply class-developed criteria to their script, analyze a videotape of their performance, or comment on their growth as a presenter, they can help their parents understand their learning experiences and level of accomplishment.

Dear Parents,

We have been practising our Readers Theatre scripts and have videotaped our last performance. As a class, we have watched our performances and each child has rated his or her own performance based on the criteria.

Please take time during the next few days and watch your child's presentation (# _____ - # _____). You are welcome to watch all the presentations. They range in length from ten to twenty minutes.

Ask your child why he/she rated themselves as he/she did. Decide your rating and explain why you decided on that particular rating (evidence or reasons).

I hope you enjoy your child's presentation and find your discussion with your child informative.

Please call me if you have any questions.

Sincerely,

Note to parents

Criteria list for child and parents

Name: _____   Date: _____

Readers Theatre presentation _____

Criteria for presentation	Child's rating and comments		Parents' rating and comments	
Performance appears rehearsed	(••)	Evidence:	(••)	Evidence:
Props used enhance the performance	(••)	Evidence:	(••)	Evidence:
Audience able to SEE readers	(••)	Evidence:	(••)	Evidence:
Audience able to HEAR readers	(••)	Evidence:	(••)	Evidence:
Reader uses voice actions pace (of speech)	(••)	Evidence:	(••)	Evidence:

Rating scale	☺ 🙂 ☹	
	☺	great
	🙂	okay; could be improved
	☹	needs more practice

Videotape – Readers Theatre
Division 9

Counter # 's

0	– 106	Whale of A Tale
107	– 214	The Monkey and The Crocodile (Part 1)
214	– 320	The Monkey and The Crocodile (Part 2)
321	– 545	The Princess and The Pea
545	– 651	Dinosaur World

Reproducible master in Appendix A

✸ *Inviting, Including, and Informing Others:* PICTURES TELL THE STORY

One effective way to highlight learning is to show the child in action. The teacher takes a photograph of the child engaged in an activity during the course of the Readers Theatre activity. The child writes or dictates a caption to accompany the photograph home. The caption helps open up discussion between the parents and the child and acts as another connection between parents and the classroom.

Explanatory letter to parents, (right)

Where available, a video camera can be set up to capture students working on a Readers Theatre script and, later, performing it. The videotape can be signed out overnight or for after-school viewing. A response form and an explanatory letter to parents keeps everyone informed.

Capturing student learning

Dear Parents,

The purpose of using Readers Theatre in our classroom this term is to

- learn effective ways to use voice (projection, pitch, emphasis, inflection, enunciation, intonation, and expression)
- provide more opportunities for reading aloud
- increase confidence while speaking in front of an audience

As you view your child and his/her classmates presenting their Readers Theatre, consider you child's developing expertise and skill in these areas.

If you have any questions, please call me. I'd be pleased to speak with you.

Sincerely,

Name: _____   Date: _____
Readers Theatre title:_____

While you are watching this performance please notice

1) _____

2) _____
   _____

- -

Dear _____ ,

When watching the video I/we noticed

1) _____

2) _____

I/We would like to compliment you for

1) _____

2) _____

One piece of advice I/we have is

1) _____
   _____

Parent response to video

Reproducible master in Appendix A

10

QUESTIONS AND ANSWERS

How do I fit Readers Theatre into my already crowded curriculum?
You don't need to let Readers Theatre reduce the number of things you must do. Every curriculum area has goals related to communicating effectively and every curriculum area has content. Readers Theatre, a blend of effective communication about something (content), is a perfect tool for meeting your instructional purposes. Use Readers Theatre to teach reading, writing, listening, speaking, and viewing while teaching the content connected to science, social studies, language arts, mathematics, and all the other subject areas.

How can I include those students who are insecure and lacking in confidence in Readers Theatre?
Give students lots of opportunities to see others in action in Readers Theatre presentations. Follow this up with small parts—consider those that have a repetitive refrain. Encourage students to take scripts home to practice with siblings and/or parents. Many students really want to be a part of a cast and they will spend time practicing their part—often to the point of memorization.

It takes time to script a story and with all the other things I have to do I don't have the time. How can I find the time?
If you are finding it difficult to locate scripts, creating your own is probably the best option. Not only does it expand your students' opportunities to write for a real purpose but it also helps you assess how well they understand the plot, characters, and setting of the stories they are reading. Younger children write simple scripts by brainstorming ideas around a theme (see page 33). Older children can be taught to script their own stories from the simple to the complex, depending on their experience. Popular children's stories can be used as models and scripted by students. Buddy classes can work together to develop scripts.

If you still want to use at least some prepared scripts, propose to your colleagues that a file drawer be set aside in the office or library to store class sets of scripts that anyone can access. This reduces the amount of copying and saves unnecessary individual preparation time. In addition to the scripts included in this book, there are some excellent sources of ready-written scripts listed in the Bibliography, page 153.

How much action should I encourage in Readers Theatre presentations?
One of the difficulties of working with students on scripts is the desire of many of them to physically act. Emphasize "acting with your voice" and using a music stand (like a podium), having the students hold the sides of the stand as they read. To enhance the script, students can use simple movements, like bowing their heads down when they are out of the scene and lifting their heads when they enter a scene. They can use simple body language, such as folding their arms across the chest (to denote stubbornness), a facial grimace, or pointing. As a rule, little movement is used as the focus should be on the language of the text—at least in the early stages of Readers Theatre.

How long should I spend on any one script with a group of students?
The time Readers Theatre takes depends on the instructional purpose for which it was selected. If you want your students to experience a piece of literature in a different way, you may select a Readers Theatre script to read aloud with them. This may take only minutes. If you want your students to learn some of the performing aspects of Readers Theatre, you may choose to devote more instructional time to help them improve in this area. The time taken for Readers Theatre depends on you and your students.

How long is there from introduction of a script to presentation?
Estimate eight to ten readings for a simple Readers Theatre production, where staging is limited, and ten to twelve readings for a staged version (see chapter 6).

Should I do one script with the entire class or four or five different ones—one for each group?
When beginning work on a script with the entire class, treat it as a lesson in oral interpretation (see ideas in Chapter 3). This allows the students to learn the process. This early lesson does not have to result in a presentation; rather it allows all students—from the confident to the less confident—to learn from one another.

Once basic techniques are understood, break the class into four or five groups and give each group a different script with which to work. When the groups are ready to present to each other, they will be able to appreciate several different stories.

When the students and I both like a story and want to turn it into a script, what do I do about copyright?

In Canada and the United States, you must write the copyright holder to get permission to turn the text into a script. Most authors are pleased to grant permission because it exposes more people to their work.

Should I use microphones in a Readers Theatre presentation?

If the space is large and voices will not carry, then by all means use a microphone. But one microphone per reader is best (it helps if you can borrow extras from the music department). One microphone passed between readers is clumsy, awkward and results in a poorly presented story. If only one microphone is available, have a "stagehand" who knows the script move the microphone from reader to reader.

Is it possible to overdo the use of Readers Theatre? How much should I use it?

Yes, it is possible to overdo Readers Theatre. Use it sparingly so that children do not lose interest. It should be a technique they enjoy and want to use. You will find that the students themselves will sometimes say "That story would be a good Readers Theatre!" When you hear that, heed it. Also consider having a Readers Theatre corner where children can go during choice or reading time and read scripts together for the fun of it.

How can Readers Theatre be incorporated into a home reading program? How do I make parents/family members aware of this strategy?

A Readers Theatre script can be shared with siblings and parents. Make parents aware of this activity through class newsletters or by inviting them to an evening of Readers Theatre performed by their children. On the same evening they could read scripts with their children and team up with other families for an informal presentation of favorite scripts (see chapter 9).

I teach English as a second language. Can I use Readers Theatre in my teaching?

In Readers Theatre, oral interpretation and body language help to impart the meaning of words and phrases. This expression provides a wider context for understanding. As well, when reading parts, more fluent partners support less able readers. English-as-a-second-language and second-language teachers can make excellent use of this activity in their classrooms.

What questions do you have now?

Who could you connect with to discover the answers?

I don't understand what offstage focus *means. Can you explain it?*

Offstage focus is an advanced skill. Performers develop their expertise over time. Initially they focus their efforts on reading the script comfortably without errors. Their goal then becomes reading comfortably for an audience. Once performers gain this expertise, they are ready to incorporate an offstage focus. This means that instead of focusing their eyes on their script or audience, they focus their eyes as if they were looking at the entire cast in a mirror located behind the audience. When their character is speaking to another character, they look at one another using the imaginary mirror image. The result is that the focal point is above the audience. Using offstage focus well is an expectation for professional performers of Readers Theatre.

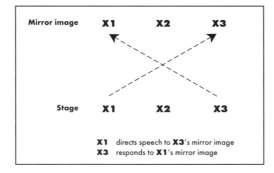

Because Readers Theatre is mainly auditory, not visual, offstage focus draws the audience into the action.

APPENDIX:
REPRODUCIBLE MASTERS

Interdisciplinary: Connections with...Language Arts, Mathematics, Social Studies, Science, Arts, Fine Arts,

Guiding Questions:

Relevant?

Connected to previous learning?

Connected to curriculum?

Connected to interests?

Interesting content?

Worth learning?

Choice for learners?

Purposeful reading, writing, communicating?

Integrates ideas and topics across subjects?

Increases skill development?

Communicates an important message?

Involves others as co-writers, co-workers, copresenters, audience?

Process

1. Write or choose a script.
2. Read script several times.
3. Work with students to allocate parts.
4. Consider props.
5. Practice.
6. Perform.

Materials needed

☐ _____

☐ _____

☐ _____

☐ _____

Script Selection

☐ Prepared script(s)

☐ Adapted literary selection(s)

☐ Student-written script(s)

Script Preparation

☐ Make copies, one for director and each reader.

☐ Highlight or underline character lines for each character.

Practical Arts, Performance Skills, Communication Skills, Self-evaluation and Goal Setting, Writing, Teamwork, Themes

From: Building Connections: Learning with Readers Theatre by Dixon/Davies/Politano © 1995. May be reproduced for classroom use.

Page 12: Planning sheet

(**Surprised**) Well, hi! I didn't know you were coming tobogganing!

(**Wistfully**) I wish she'd let me have one more piece of birthday cake.

(**Bellowing**) Get out of there...and don't come back, do you hear me?

(**Angrily**) I told you to go to your room. Now will you do as you're told?

(**Frightened**) Who is it? Who's there? Don't come near me...Don't! Don't!

(**Whispering**) What's the surprise? You can tell me. I won't tell.

(**Quiet, secretive voice**) Be quiet. I don't think they can hear us, but we'd better be sure.

(**Eagerly**) You mean, it's my turn now?

(**Hysterical with worry**) I didn't mean to hurt her. She's my best friend!

(**Hysterically happy**) I won! I won! First prize...I won!

(**Nervously**) We're going to get caught. I tell you. Come on, let's get out of here. It's dangerous, I tell you. Come on!

(**Aghast**) It's been hit. That car ran right over that deer.

Hint: This can be used as a handout, or prepared as individual sentence sentence strips. Enlarge sheets to 11" x 17 on the photocopier, then laminate and cut between sentences.

Page 15: Vocal-coloring sentences

The wild wind whipped what from the wharf.

A black-backed bath brush

Tom threw Tim three thumbtacks.

This thistle seems like that thistle.

The seething sea ceaseth seething.

Old oily Ollie oils oily Oldsmobiles.

The big black-backed bumblebee

Rubber baby buggy bumpers

She says she will sew a sheet.

Toy boat

Double bubble gum bubbles double.

A noisy noise annoys an oyster.

Far dogs frying fritters and fiddling ferociously

Brisk brave brigadiers brandished broad blades, blunderbusses, and bludgeons.

Wise wives whistle while weaving worsted waistcoats.

A tooter who tooted a flute
Tried to tutor two tutors to toot.
Said the two to the tootor,
"Is it harder to toot
Or to tutor two tutors to toot?"

The big black bug bit the big black bear and made the big black bear bleed blood.

The skunk sat on a stump and thunk the stump stunk, but the stump thunk the skunk stunk.

A pale pink proud peacock pompously preened its pretty plumage.

Page 20: Tongue twisters

butcher	lawyer	carpenter
painter	writer	farmer
fisher	police officer	flight attendant
hair stylist	pilot	actor
teenager	gardener	horse rider
soccer field	mall	country farm
hotel	classroom	house
boat cruise	ship	theater
broken water pipes	angry dog	hole in the boat
flat tire	head wind	empty box

Page 27: Character, setting, and problem cards

Name: _____ **Date:** _____

Title: _____

Characters: _____ **Readers:** _____

_____ _____

_____ _____

_____ _____

_____ _____

_____ _____

Reader _____ : _____

_____

Reader _____ : _____

_____

Reader _____ : _____

_____

Reader _____ : _____

_____

Reader _____ : _____

_____

Reader _____ : _____

_____

Page 65: Script master, page 1

Reader _____ : _____

_____

Reader _____ : _____

_____

Reader _____ : _____

_____

Reader _____ : _____

_____

Reader _____ : _____

_____

Reader _____ : _____

_____

Reader _____ : _____

_____

Reader _____ : _____

_____

Reader _____ : _____

_____

Reader _____ : _____

_____

Reader _____ : _____

_____

Reader _____ : _____

_____

Page 65: Script master, page 2

Name _____ **Date** _____ **Class** _____

What I want you to notice: _____
_____

Criteria	✔	Student Observation/Comment
1. _____		_____
_____		_____
2. _____		_____
_____		_____
3. _____		_____
_____		_____
4. _____		_____
_____		_____

You should know: _____
_____

Name _____ **Date** _____ **Class** _____

What I want you to notice: _____
_____

Criteria	✔	Student Observation/Comment
1. _____		_____
_____		_____
2. _____		_____
_____		_____
3. _____		_____
_____		_____
4. _____		_____
_____		_____

You should know: _____
_____

Page 72: Student evaluation checklist

Name _____   **Date** _____

Today we _____
_____

The part I enjoy the most is _____
_____

The part I am best at is _____
_____

The part I most want to improve in is _____
_____

Next time I'd like to _____
_____
_____

Name _____   **Date** _____

Three things I know about my character are
_____
_____
_____

My character begins feeling _____
and ends feeling _____

My character's role can be described by the following words: _____
_____
_____
_____
_____
_____
_____

Page 74: Self-assessment frames

Name _____ **Date** _____

The language in my script is powerful because _____
_____

There is a balance between narration and dialogue. I can prove this by _____
_____

The dialogue has a good pace. I know this because _____
_____

This script is written for a _____ reader. I know that this kind of reader can read this script. My proof is _____
_____

The directions are clear. For example _____
_____

This script could be improved by _____
_____

Next time I write a script I will _____
_____

Name _____ **Date** _____

I have been practicing my reading of the script called _____
_____

I have been practicing with _____
_____

I read this script _____ .
I know this because _____
_____

I use body language when _____
_____

I use vocal coloring when _____
_____

I could improve my script reading by _____
_____

Next time I am read a script I will _____
_____

Page 74: Self-assessment frames

Name _____ **Date** _____

I'm focusing on the following criteria for an effective Readers Theatre performance:

_____   _____

_____   _____

_____   _____

I know I have improved/met the criteria because when you watch the video of my performance you'll notice

1. _____

   _____

   _____

2. _____

   _____

   _____

3. _____

   _____

   _____

Parent Comment

Dear _____ ,

We just want you to know that _____

and next time please _____

Page 74: Video evaluation form

Group Self-Report

Members _____ **Date** _____

_____

Task _____

The best part of working together was _____

_____

_____

_____

The part we need to improve the most is _____

_____

_____

_____

One problem we had was _____

_____

_____

_____

We solved it by _____

_____

_____

_____

signed _____

_____

Page 75: Group self-reporting frame

Name _____ **Date** _____ **to** _____

Group Members

_____

_____

_____

Rating Criteria

1. Rarely observed
2. Sometimes observed
3. Frequently observed
   (becoming characteristic of students)

Readers Theatre Presentation of _____	Group Self-Rating 1 2 3	Comments Student	Teacher
1.	☐ ☐ ☐		
2.	☐ ☐ ☐		
3.	☐ ☐ ☐		
4.	☐ ☐ ☐		
5.	☐ ☐ ☐		
6.	☐ ☐ ☐		
7.	☐ ☐ ☐		

Summary Comments

Page 76: Group rating form

Name _____ **Date** _____

Script title

_____

Rating

Yes, I'm doing well
No, I need to improve

Criteria for _____ _____ _____	Rating scale yes/no	Self-Evaluation Comment on your script reading	Ask someone else to comment on your script reading

I am pleased because _____

_____

My next steps for improving are _____

_____

Page 76: Rating form

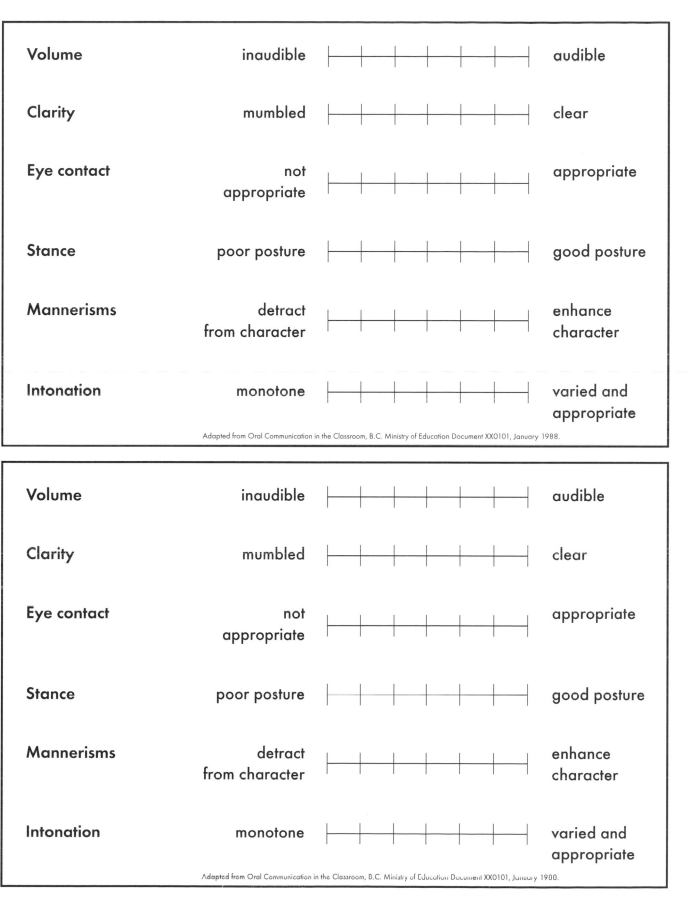

Volume	inaudible	audible
Clarity	mumbled	clear
Eye contact	not appropriate	appropriate
Stance	poor posture	good posture
Mannerisms	detract from character	enhance character
Intonation	monotone	varied and appropriate

Adapted from Oral Communication in the Classroom, B.C. Ministry of Education Document XX0101, January 1988.

Volume	inaudible	audible
Clarity	mumbled	clear
Eye contact	not appropriate	appropriate
Stance	poor posture	good posture
Mannerisms	detract from character	enhance character
Intonation	monotone	varied and appropriate

Adapted from Oral Communication in the Classroom, B.C. Ministry of Education Document XX0101, January 1988.

Page 76: Rating form

Personal Storytelling Record

Name _____

Story Name	Content	Where I found it	Who I told it to	When I told it

Readers Theatre Participation Record

Name _____ Date _____

Readers theatre title _____

My part _____

My group members _____

Director _____

Comment _____

_____

Page 77: Personal storytelling record; page 77: Readers Theatre participation record

NEWSLETTER

Dear Parent(s):

During the past month we have been using Readers Theatre as a strategy to help students become better readers and better communicators. The script that follows will explain the basics of Readers Theatre and show how Readers Theatre is used in the classroom.

In the school setting, Readers Theatre may be used in many different ways. It is an excellent reading strategy, helping students understand characters and their feelings. It can also be used in other subjects to explain processes or concepts. It is a versatile strategy—children can build scripts around a theme or take a story they have written and turn it into a script to be shared by their classmates.

Readers Theatre encourages clear projection, good expression, variety of tone and pitch, and fluency in reading. It may be staged for presentation purposes. This may involve readers being at different levels, standing on risers, sitting on stools or chairs, or kneeling. It may be read by a group in the corner of the classroom purely for the participants' enjoyment. Poetry, songs, letters, plays, and short stories can all be turned into scripts for Readers Theatre.

Readers Theatre is a simple, yet effective classroom learning strategy. Get ready! Your child will organize and direct you and your family during your first Readers Theatre performance. Have fun!

Sincerely,

Readers Theatre Goes Home

Roles for Readers	Names
Parent 1/Narrator 1	_____
Parent 2/Narrator 2	_____
Child 1/Mother Bear	_____
Child 2/Father Bear	_____
Child 3/Baby Bear and Goldilocks	_____

Child 1:	We did Readers Theatre today
Parent 1:	What's Readers Theatre?
Child 2:	It's reading a story
Child 2:	in parts.
Parent 1:	What do you mean in parts?
Child 1:	We could be characters
Child 3:	or narrators,
Child 2:	acting with our voices.
Parent 1:	How do you act with your voice?
Child 2:	We have to understand the character...
Child 3:	how the character feels,
Child 2:	thinks,
Child 1:	and acts.
Parent 1:	So you read clearly
Child 3:	and with good expression
Parent 2:	as though you really are the character
Parent 1:	and are acting the way that character feels.
Parent 2:	Do you have a story to show how Readers Theatre works?
Child 2:	Yes, we have a fairy tale we adapted for Readers Theatre.
Child 1:	Dad, you read the part of Narrator 2
Child 3:	and Mom you read Narrator 1.
Child 1:	I'll read Father Bear.
Child 2:	I'll be Mother Bear,
Child 3:	while I read the part of Baby Bear and Goldilocks.
Narrator 1:	Once upon a time there were three bears.
Narrator 2:	There was a father, mother, and a baby.
Narrator 1:	They lived in a little house in the woods.
Narrator 2:	One morning, after Mother Bear had made the breakfast she suggested,
Mother Bear:	Let's go for a walk while the porridge cools.
Father Bear:	Yes, we can enjoy the morning by walking in the woods,
Narrator 1:	said Father Bear.
Narrator 2:	They left the house.
Baby Bear:	It's nice out walking today.

Page 86: Newsletter, page 2

Narrator 1:	While they were out a little girl with golden hair wandered by their house.
Narrator 2:	She could smell the breakfast and decided to go inside.
Narrator 1:	She saw the porridge.
Goldilocks:	I think I'll try some of that,
Narrator 2:	said Goldilocks.
Narrator 1:	She tried the first bowl.
Goldilocks:	Oh, too hot!
Narrator 2:	she exclaimed and tried the second bowl.
Narrator 1:	She tried the third.
Goldilocks:	Just right! I'll eat it all!
Narrator 2:	After that she wandered around the house looking at everything.
Narrator 1:	Then she sat in Father Bear's big chair.
Goldilocks:	Too hard and uncomfortable. I'll try this middle-sized chair.
Narrator 2:	She sat down.
Goldilocks:	Too soft!
Narrator 1:	Then she sat on the smallest chair.
Goldilocks:	Just right! So comfortable. Oops!
Narrator 2:	As she sat down, one of the legs broke off the chair.
Narrator 1:	Goldilocks got up and went into the bedroom.
Narrator 2:	She lay down on Father Bear's bed.
Goldilocks:	Too lumpy and hard.
Narrator 1:	She tried Mother Bear's bed.
Goldilocks:	Too soft.
Narrator 2:	She tried Baby bear's bed.
Goldilocks:	Just right...so-o-o comfortable,
Narrator 1:	and she fell asleep.
Narrator 2:	When the bears arrived back they could tell someone had been in their home.
Father Bear:	Who's been eating my porridge?
Narrator 1:	growled Father Bear.
Mother Bear:	Who's been eating my porridge?
Narrator 2:	grumbled Mother Bear.
Baby Bear:	Who's been eating my porridge? It's all gone!
Narrator 1:	squealed Baby Bear.
Father Bear:	Who's been sitting in my chair?
Narrator 2:	growled Father Bear.
Mother Bear:	Who's been sitting in my chair?
Narrator 1:	grumbled Mother Bear.
Baby Bear:	Who's been sitting in my chair and broken it?
Narrator 2:	squealed Baby Bear, and he started to cry.
Father Bear:	Who's been lying in my bed?
Narrator 1:	growled Father Bear.
Mother Bear:	Who's been lying on my bed?
Narrator 2:	grumbled Mother Bear.
Baby Bear:	Someone's been lying on my bed and she's still here!
Narrator 1:	squealed Baby Bear.
Narrator 2:	Goldilocks woke and sat up
Goldilocks:	Oh, help!

Page 86: Newsletter, page 3

Narrator 1:	she screamed, and ran out of the house.
Narrator 2:	The bears looked at her running off.
Mother Bear:	We won't bother to chase after her.
Baby Bear:	She looked so scared I'm sure she learned a lesson.
Father Bear:	Let's go and eat breakfast. Mother Bear, will you make some more porridge? (*Mother Bear nods*)
Narrator 2:	Father Bear helped Baby Bear repair his chair and Goldilocks never again went into a house without being invited.

Criteria for Effective Readers Theatre

In our classroom this term our skills emphasis has been on being a "good reader" as we perform Readers Theatre. Other times during the year we may focus on scriptwriting or presenting Readers Theatre. Each area of Readers Theatre develops different skills.

What makes a good reader in Readers Theatre?

- Uses voice effectively (projection, pitch, emphasis, inflection, enunciation, intonation, expression)
- Familiar with the script/able to read the material
- Knows his/her own place in the script
- Demonstrates confidence and enthusiasm
- Uses actions to enhance the presentation
- Recognizes cues and can pace him/herself effectively

- -

Readers Theatre: Thinking About My Learning

Name: _____

Date: _____

I am improving as a reader in Readers Theatre. I know this because:

In order to improve even more I need to:

What do you think?

From: *Building Connections: Learning with Readers Theatre* by Dixon/Davies/Politano © 1995. May be reproduced for classroom use.

Page 86: Newsletter, page 4

Name: _____ Date: _____

Readers Theatre presentation _____

Criteria for presentation	Child's rating and comments	Parents' rating and comments
	Evidence:	Evidence:
	Evidence:	Evidence:
	Evidence:	Evidence:
	Evidence:	Evidence:
	Evidence:	Evidence:

Rating scale		
	great
	okay; could be improved
	needs more practice

From: Building Connections: Learning with Readers Theatre by Dixon/Davies/Politano © 1995. May be reproduced for classroom use.

Page 87: Criteria list for child and parent(s)

Name: _____ **Date:** _____

Readers Theatre title: _____

While you are watching this performance please notice

1) _____

_____

2) _____

_____

- -

Dear _____ ,

When watching the video I/we noticed

1) _____

_____

2) _____

_____

I/We would like to compliment you for

1) _____

_____

2) _____

_____

One piece of advice I/we have is

1) _____

_____

From: Building Connections: *Learning with Readers Theatre* by Dixon/Davies/Politano © 1995. May be reproduced for classroom use.

Page 88: Parent response to video

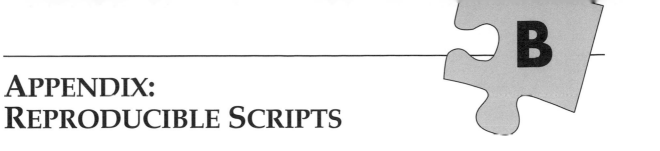

APPENDIX:
REPRODUCIBLE SCRIPTS

Note: The scripts in this section can be reproduced, or changed and adapted by readers for their own situations.

The Princess and the Pea *

Characters	Readers
Narrator 1	_____
Narrator 2	_____
Prince	_____
Girl	_____
Queen	_____
King	_____

Narrator 1: Once upon a time there was a prince who traveled far.

Narrator 2: He traveled far for many months, searching for a princess to marry.

Narrator 1: The prince met many young ladies who said they were princesses,

Narrator 2: but he was not sure they were telling the truth.

Prince: I was most unhappy when I returned to the family castle.

Narrator 1: One night there was a storm,

Narrator 2: a terrible storm!

Queen: With all this thunder and lightning, I'm sure glad we're inside.

Narrator 1: Suddenly, there was a loud knock on the palace door.

Narrator 2: The king answered it.

Narrator 1: Standing at the door was a strange girl.

Girl: Good evening, sir. I've lost my way and I'm cold and wet. May I come in and rest awhile?

King: Of course, my dear, come in at once. You must stay until the storm is over.

Girl: Oh, thank you sir.

Narrator 2: The girl entered and began to dry off and warm up.

Queen: Have some supper, dear. You must be hungry.

Girls: Yes, I am. Thank you, you are so kind.

King: How did you happen to get caught in the storm?

Girl: I was out walking early in the evening. I had wandered far away from the castle (you see, I'm a princess), further than I ever had before, and when the storm happened, I became confused.

* adapted for Readers Theatre by Beth Mole

Page 38: Princess and Pea, page 1

Prince:	(aside) She says she's a princess. Of all the girls I have met, this is the one I want to believe.
Narrator 1:	The queen, who was very wise, went off to make up the guest bed.
Narrator 2:	She did not tell anyone what she did, but she put a pea on the wooden slats of the bed.
Queen:	On top of the pea I put many mattresses and feather pillows.
Narrator 1:	The girl had to climb almost to the ceiling to get into the bed!
Narrator 2:	Next morning the queen said,
Queen:	Did you sleep well my dear?
Girl:	Oh no, hardly at all. The bed was very lumpy. I tossed and turned all night.
Queen:	Come with me, my dear.
Narrator 1:	And the queen took her to the prince.
Queen:	Only a real princess would be unable to sleep because of a pea under such a pile of pillows and mattresses.
Narrator 2:	The queen explained what she had done.
Queen:	You see, I placed a pea between the slats and bottom mattress and then piled all the other mattresses on top...
King:	...and of course, as you said, only a real princess would find the bed uncomfortable.
Prince:	That was a good test, mother. Thank you. This makes me very happy, as I could wish for nothing more than to have this princess as my wife.
Princess:	I am happy, too. I accept your proposal.
Narrator 1:	The prince and his newfound princess were married...
Narrator 2:	...and of course they lived happily ever after.

Page 38: Princess and Pea, *page 2*

Grandfather's Memories *

Final Draft

For four readers

Narrator 1: Over supper Grandfather was still remembering...

Grandfather: *Hmmm, your grandmother's fresh baking...that was one of the things that kept us going that winter,*

Narrator 1: *he recalled.*

Grandmother: But even home baking had its dangers,

Narrator 2: Grandmother continued.

Grandmother: One afternoon I was baking pies...

Grandfather: and she ran out of raisins,

Narrator 1: Grandfather interrupted.

Narrator 1: *Grandfather was sent to the neighbors' to borrow some.*

Grandmother: Get bundled up before you head out into the cold,

Narrator 2: *Grandmother shivered as she remembered.*

Grandfather: *You bet,*

Narrator 1: *replied Grandfather.*

Grandfather: *She stood in the door waving to me*

Narrator 1: *Grandfather told how he left and then said*

Grandfather: Of course without thinking I turned and blew her a kiss.

Narrator 1: *Grandfather wasn't thinking when he blew the kiss!*

Narrator 2: *Because of the severe cold...*

All: *How cold?*

Grandmother: So cold that the kiss froze into a solid lump

Grandfather: before it got halfway to the house.

Narrator 1: *added Grandfather.*

Narrator 2: *That solid kiss hit Grandmother full force...*

All: *Whack!*

*adapted from Cold Night, Brittle Light, by Richard Thompson, © 1994, Orca Book Publishers.

Page 42: Grandfather's Memories, page 1

Grandmother:	*Right* on my forehead
Narrator 2:	It knocked Grandmother senseless
Grandmother:	for the better part of the day
Narrator 2:	*and then she added*
Grandmother:	I never did get those pies done.
Narrator 1:	The cold that winter caused a few problems
Narrator 2:	for the folks in town, too.
Grandfather:	It was so cold
All:	*How cold?*
Narrator 1:	*And Grandfather responded*
Grandfather:	that when people's breath came out it froze solid
Narrator 2:	*Grandmother added*
Grandmother:	A person had to break off one breath and throw it down on the ground before he could take another one.
Narrator 1:	Lumps of frozen breath all over the streets.
Grandfather:	It wasn't long before you could hardly move downtown
Grandmother:	for the piles of breath every place you turned.

Page 42: Grandfather's Memories, *page 2*

Ladies First

by Shel Silverstein
Adapted for Readers Theatre

Roles for Readers	Student Names
Narrator 1	_____
Narrator 2	_____
Lady	_____
Chief Tiger	_____
Tigers (2 or 3)	_____
	_____
	_____

Enter from stage right, carrying scripts under right arm, Narrator 2 leads, followed by Tiger 2, Chief Tiger, Tiger 1, Lady, Narrator 1. All take positions behind their music stands. Three tigers lower their heads to show they are out of the scene.

Narrators use audience focus, characters use offstage focus.

Suggested Staging

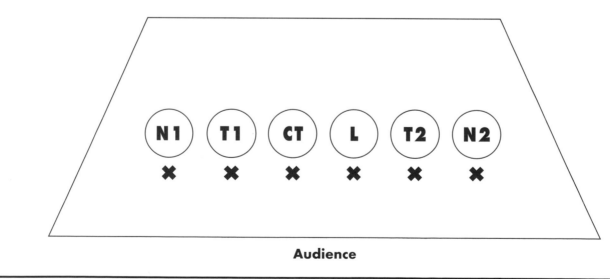

Page 45: Ladies First, *simple version, page 1*

Narrator 2:	Ladies First, by Shel Silverstein.
Narrator 1:	Did you hear the one about the little girl who was the "tender, sweet young thing"? Well, that's the way she thought of herself.
Narrator 2:	And this tender sweet young thing spent a great deal of time just looking in the mirror, saying:
Lady:	(*indicates each item by pointing*) I am a real little lady. Anybody could tell that. I wear lovely, starched cotton dresses with matching ribbons in my lovely, curly locks. I wear clean white socks and black, shiny patent-leather shoes, and I always put just a dab of perfume behind my ear.
Narrator 2:	When she was at the end of the lunch line in school all she had to say was...
Lady:	Ladies first, ladies first...
Narrator 1:	and she'd get right up to the front of the line. (*Lady smiles victoriously*)
Narrator 2:	Well, her life went on like that for quite a while and she wound up having a pretty good time—you know—admiring herself in mirrors, always getting to be first in line, and stuff like that.
Narrator 1:	And then one day, she went exploring with a whole group of other people through the wilds of a deep and beastly jungle. As she went along through the tangled trails and prickly vines, she would say things like:
Lady:	(*indicates each item by pointing*) I have got to be careful of my lovely dress and my nice white socks and my shiny, shiny shoes and my curly, curly locks. So would somebody please clear the way for me?
Narrator 1:	And they did.
Narrator 2:	Or sometimes she'd say...
Lady:	What-do-you-mean there aren't enough mangoes to go around, and I'll have to share my mango—because I was the last one across the icky river full of crocodiles and snakes?
Lady:	No matter how last I am, it's still "Ladies first, ladies first", so (*harshly*) hand over a whole mango, (*softly, pleasantly*) please!!!
Narrator 2:	And they did.
Narrator 1:	Well then, guess what happened?

Page 45: Ladies First, *simple version, page 2*

Narrator 2:	Suddenly the exploring party was seized (*Tigers lift heads and sniff around*) by the tigers and dragged back to their lair, where the tigers sniffed around, trying to decide what would make the best dinner.
Chief Tiger:	How about this one? (*Focus audience left*)
Tigers:	Naah, too bony...
Chief Tiger:	What about this one? (*Focus audience right*)
Tigers:	Uh-unh, meaty, but too muscle-y.
Chief Tiger:	Oh, for heaven's sake, don't take all night,
Narrator 2:	said the Chief Tiger
Chief Tiger:	I never saw such a pack of picky eaters! How about this one (*focus down in front of Lady*) then? It looks tender, and smells nice. In fact, I never saw anything quite like this before. I wonder what it is?
Lady:	I am a sweet young thing (*focus up in front of Chief Tiger*).
Narrator 1:	She said
Chief Tiger:	Oh, far out!
Narrator 2:	said the Tiger Chief.
Lady:	I'm also a little lady. You should know that by my lovely clothes and my lovely smell. And if it's all the same to you, Tiger Tweetie, I wish you'd (*harshly*) stop licking me and untie me this instant. (*Pleasantly*) My dress is getting mussed.
Chief Tiger:	Yes...Well, as a matter of fact, we were all just trying to decide who to untie first.
Lady:	Ladies first! Ladies first!
Narrator 1:	she said,
Narrator 2:	and so she was. (*Lady lowers head to be out of scene*)
All Tigers:	AND MIGHTY TASTY, TOO !!!

(*Lady lifts head and all readers place scripts under right arm and turn to face stage right, led off by Narrator 1, the others follow in this order: Narrator 1, Tiger 1, Chief Tiger, Lady, Tiger 2, and Narrator 2*)

Page 45: Ladies First, *simple version, page 3*

Ladies First

by Shel Silverstein
Adapted for Readers Theatre

Roles for Readers	Student Names
Narrator 1	_____
Narrator 2	_____
Lady	_____
Chief Tiger	_____
Tigers (2 or 3)	_____
	_____
	_____

Formal entrance from stage right with scripts under right arms in the following order: Narrator 2, Tiger 2, Chief Tiger, Tiger 1, Lady, Narrator

Chief Tiger stands on chair at center stage. Other tigers on floor flanking Chief. Narrator 1 and Narrator 2 behind music stands. All face front until Narrator 1 removes script to reading position. Other characters follow and tigers right about turn to have their backs to the audience.

Suggested Staging

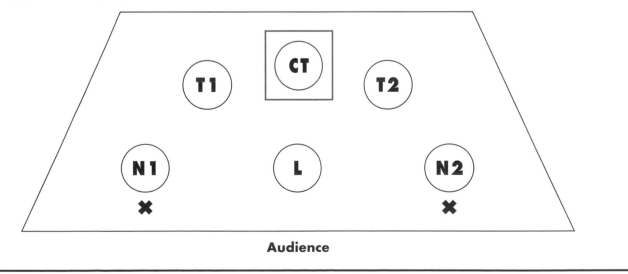

Page 47: Ladies First, *fully staged version, page 1*

Narrator 2	Ladies First, by Shel Silverstein.

(Audience eye contact)

Narrator 1:	(*Addressing Narrator 2 on stage left*) Did you hear the one about the little girl who was the "tender sweet young thing"? (*Addresses audience*) Well, that's the way she thought of herself.
Narrator 2:	(*Addressing audience*) And this tender sweet young thing spent a great deal of time just looking in the mirror, saying:
Lady:	I am a *real* little lady. Anybody could tell that. (*Gestures to dress*) I wear lovely starched cotton dresses with matching (*flicks hair*) ribbons in my lovely, curly locks. I wear clean white (*indicate feet*) socks and black, shiny patent-leather shoes and I always (*dab perfume*) put just a dab of perfume behind each ear.
Narrator 2:	When she was at the end of the lunch line in school all she had to say was...
Lady:	(*Politely*) Ladies first, (*harshly*) ladies first (*repeat line with different emphasis*),
Narrator 1:	and she'd get right up to the front of the line (*Lady shows how pleased she is*).
Narrator 2:	Well, her life went on like that for quite a while and she wound up having a pretty good time (*Lady looks smug*)—you know—(*Lady mimes these actions*) admiring herself in mirrors, always getting to be first in line, and stuff like that...
Narrator 1:	and then one day, she went exploring with a whole group of other people through the wilds of a (*Lady shows distaste*) deep and beastly jungle. As she went along through the tangled trails and prickly vines, she would say things like:
Lady:	(*Indicating each*) I have got to be careful of my lovely dress and my nice white socks and my shiny, shiny shoes and my curly, curly locks. So would somebody (*harshly*) **please** (*nicely*) clear the way for me?
Narrator 1:	And they did.
Narrator 2:	Or sometimes she'd say:
Lady:	What-do-you-mean there aren't enough mangoes to go around, and I'll have to share my mango—because I was the last one across that icky river full of crocodiles and snakes? No matter how last I am, it's still "Ladies first, (*harshly*)ladies first", (*Point script towards audience*) so (*sternly*) hand over a whole mango, (*pleasantly*) please!!!
Narrator 2:	and they did.
Narrator 1:	Well then, guess what happened?

Page 47: Ladies First, fully staged version, page 2

Narrator 2:	Suddenly the exploring party was seized (*Tigers turn right to face front*) by the tigers and dragged back to their lair, where the tigers sniffed (*Tigers sniff air and make hungry, lip-smacking sounds*) around, trying to decide what would make the best dinner.
Chief Tiger:	How about this one (*pointing off stage left to a person in the audience*)?
Narrator 1:	said the Chief tiger
Tigers:	(*Turning towards the selected audience member*) Naah, too bony...
Chief Tiger:	What about this one (*pointing off stage right to another audience member*)?
Tigers:	(*Turning towards the selected member of the audience*) Uh-unh, meaty, but too muscle-y.
Chief Tiger:	I never saw such a pack of picky eaters! How about this one (*looking down and pointing to a person in the front row*) then? It looks tender, (*sniffing and licking*) and smells nice. In fact, I never saw anything quite like this before. I wonder what it is.
Lady:	(*Looking towards ceiling above the position pointed to by the chief tiger*) I am a sweet young thing,
Narrator 1:	she said.
Chief Tiger:	Oh, far out!
Narrator 2:	said the Tiger chief.
Lady:	I'm also a little lady. You should know that by my lovely clothes and my lovely smell. And if it's all the same to you, Tiger Tweetie, I wish you'd (*sternly*) stop licking me and untie me, this instant. (*Pleasantly*) My dress is getting mussed.
Chief Tiger:	Yes...Well, as a matter of fact, we were all just trying to decide who to untie first.
Lady:	Ladies first! (*Emphasize ladies in the repeated line*) Ladies first!
Narrator 1:	she said.
Narrator 2:	And so she was! (*Lady turns her back towards the audience*)
All Tigers:	AND MIGHTY TASTY, TOO!

Pause for count of three, then Lady turns front.

All place scripts under right arms, then all turn stage right and, led by N1, walk off stage in the following order: N1, Tiger 1, Lady, Chief Tiger, Tiger 2, and Narrator 2.

Page 47: Ladies First, *fully staged version, page 3*

Seashore

Roles for Readers   **Student Names**

Reader 1   _____

Reader 2   _____

Reader 3   _____

Reader 4   _____

Reader 5   _____

Suggested Staging

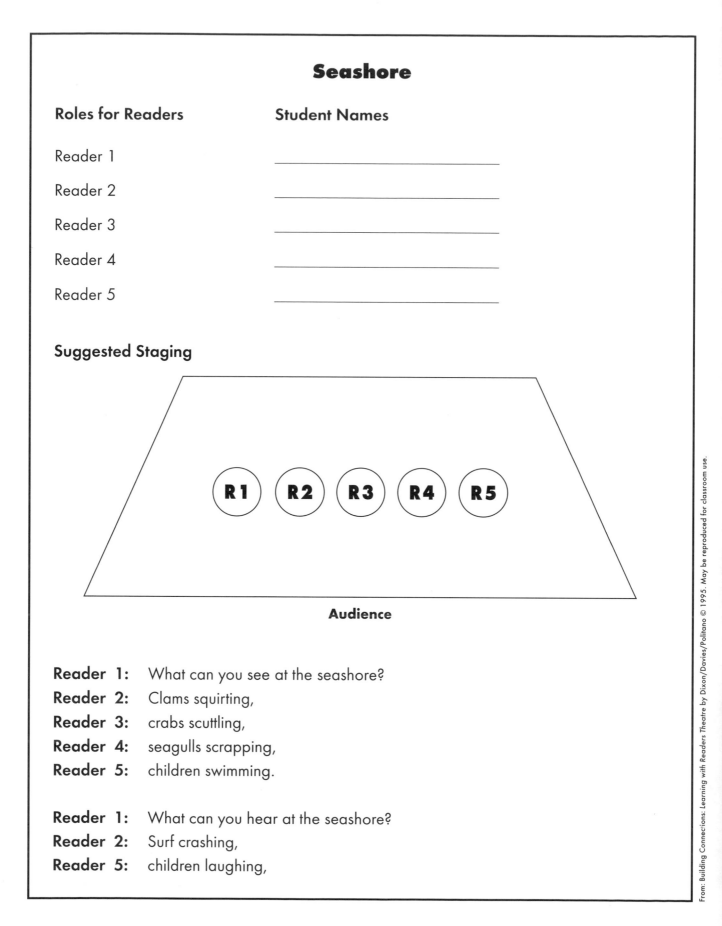

Audience

Reader 1: What can you see at the seashore?
Reader 2: Clams squirting,
Reader 3: crabs scuttling,
Reader 4: seagulls scrapping,
Reader 5: children swimming.

Reader 1: What can you hear at the seashore?
Reader 2: Surf crashing,
Reader 5: children laughing,

Page 54: Theme script: Seashore, *page 1*

| Reader 3: | waves lapping, |
| Reader 2: | seabirds calling. |

Reader 1:	What do you smell at the seashore?
Reader 3:	Salty air,
Reader 4:	seaweed,
Reader 5:	suntan lotion,
Reader 2:	smoke from the fire.

Reader 5:	I like to swim with the incoming tide.
Reader 3:	I like to relax in the sun.
Reader 1:	I like to sleep on the beach logs.
Reader 2:	I like to read.
Reader 4:	I like to look for shells.
Reader 2:	I like to listen to the water lapping.
Reader 3:	I like to explore.
Reader 5:	I like to snorkel.
Reader 1:	I like to play volleyball on the sand.
Reader 4:	I like to put my ear to the conch shell.

| All: | We hear the seashore calling. |

Page 54: Theme script: Seashore, *page 2*

Purpose

Roles for Readers   **Student Names**

Reader 1   _____

Reader 2   _____

Reader 3   _____

Suggested Staging

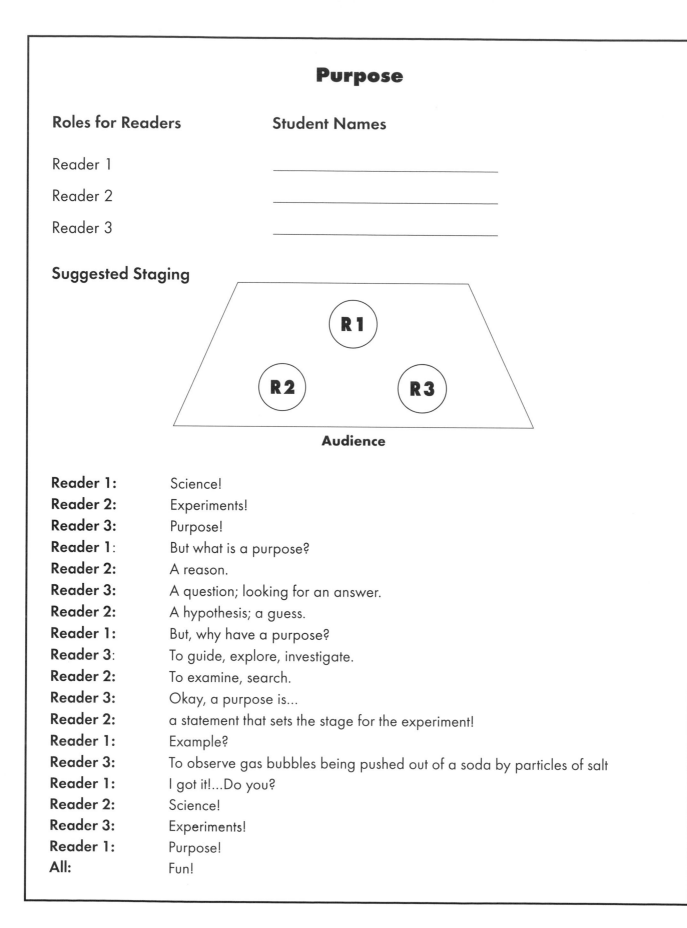

Audience

Reader 1:	Science!
Reader 2:	Experiments!
Reader 3:	Purpose!
Reader 1:	But what is a purpose?
Reader 2:	A reason.
Reader 3:	A question; looking for an answer.
Reader 2:	A hypothesis; a guess.
Reader 1:	But, why have a purpose?
Reader 3:	To guide, explore, investigate.
Reader 2:	To examine, search.
Reader 3:	Okay, a purpose is...
Reader 2:	a statement that sets the stage for the experiment!
Reader 1:	Example?
Reader 3:	To observe gas bubbles being pushed out of a soda by particles of salt
Reader 1:	I got it!...Do you?
Reader 2:	Science!
Reader 3:	Experiments!
Reader 1:	Purpose!
All:	Fun!

Page 54: Science script: Purpose

Materials

Roles for Readers　　**Student Names**

Reader 1　　　　　_____

Reader 2　　　　　_____

Reader 3　　　　　_____

Suggested Staging

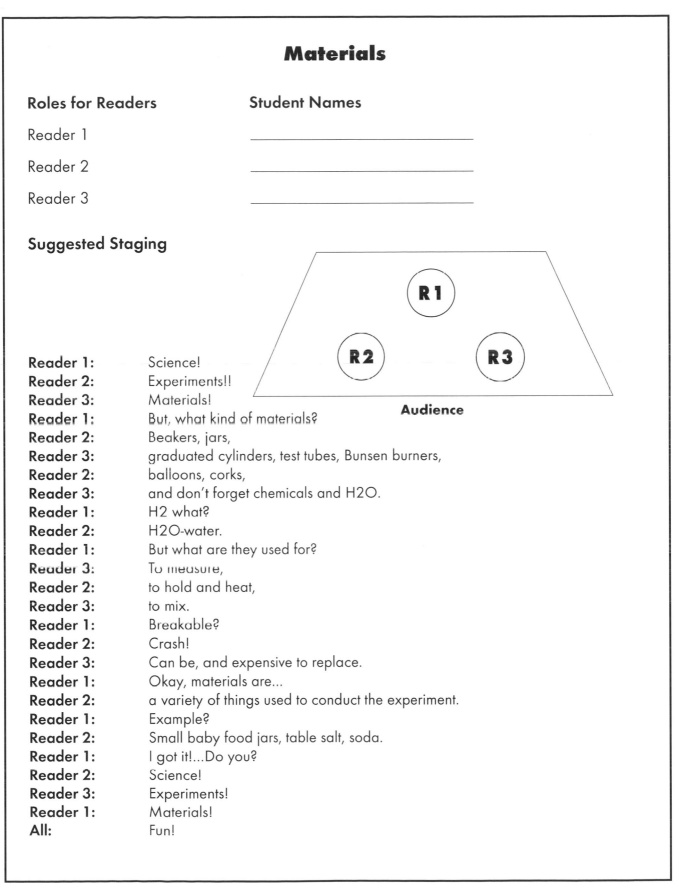

Reader 1:	Science!
Reader 2:	Experiments!!
Reader 3:	Materials!
Reader 1:	But, what kind of materials?
Reader 2:	Beakers, jars,
Reader 3:	graduated cylinders, test tubes, Bunsen burners,
Reader 2:	balloons, corks,
Reader 3:	and don't forget chemicals and H2O.
Reader 1:	H2 what?
Reader 2:	H2O–water.
Reader 1:	But what are they used for?
Reader 3:	To measure,
Reader 2:	to hold and heat,
Reader 3:	to mix.
Reader 1:	Breakable?
Reader 2:	Crash!
Reader 3:	Can be, and expensive to replace.
Reader 1:	Okay, materials are...
Reader 2:	a variety of things used to conduct the experiment.
Reader 1:	Example?
Reader 2:	Small baby food jars, table salt, soda.
Reader 1:	I got it!...Do you?
Reader 2:	Science!
Reader 3:	Experiments!
Reader 1:	Materials!
All:	Fun!

Page 57: Science script: Materials

Observations

Roles for Readers   **Student Names**

Reader 1   _____

Reader 2   _____

Reader 3   _____

Suggested Staging

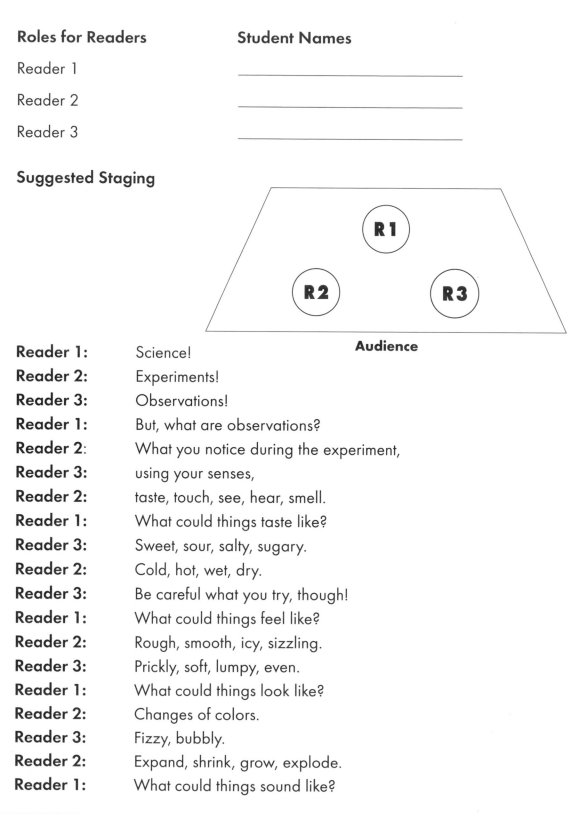

Audience

Reader 1:	Science!
Reader 2:	Experiments!
Reader 3:	Observations!
Reader 1:	But, what are observations?
Reader 2:	What you notice during the experiment,
Reader 3:	using your senses,
Reader 2:	taste, touch, see, hear, smell.
Reader 1:	What could things taste like?
Reader 3:	Sweet, sour, salty, sugary.
Reader 2:	Cold, hot, wet, dry.
Reader 3:	Be careful what you try, though!
Reader 1:	What could things feel like?
Reader 2:	Rough, smooth, icy, sizzling.
Reader 3:	Prickly, soft, lumpy, even.
Reader 1:	What could things look like?
Reader 2:	Changes of colors.
Reader 3:	Fizzy, bubbly.
Reader 2:	Expand, shrink, grow, explode.
Reader 1:	What could things sound like?

Page 57: Science script: Observations, *page 1*

Reader 2:	Loud, silent, crunch, slither.
Reader 3:	Crumple, creak, bang, pop.
Reader 1:	What could things smell like?
Reader 2:	Nothing—or a powerful smell.
Reader 3:	Rotten eggs or perfume.
Reader 2:	Be careful if you have a sensitive nose!
Reader 1:	Okay, observations are...
Reader 2:	using the senses to state what is happening during the experiment.
Reader 1:	Example?
Reader 3:	Fizzing, overflowing, bubbling.
Reader 1:	I got it!...Do you?
Reader 2	Science!
Reader 3	Experiments!
Reader 1	Observations!
All:	Fun!

Page 57: Science script: Observations, *page 2*

Method

Roles for Readers

Reader 1

Reader 2

Reader 3

Student Names

_____

_____

_____

Suggested Staging

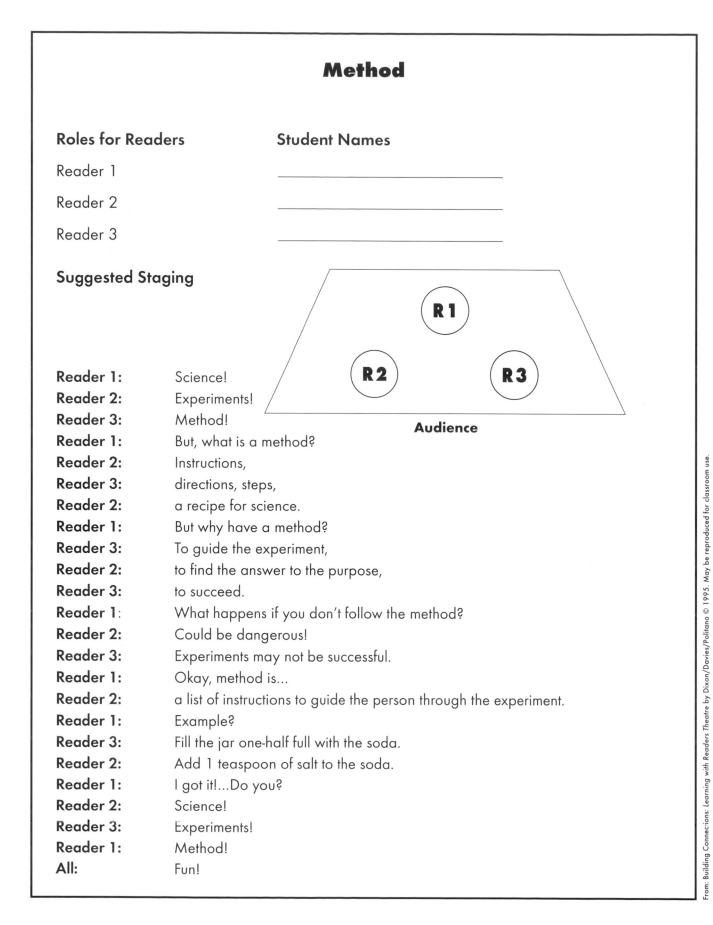

Audience

Reader 1:	Science!
Reader 2:	Experiments!
Reader 3:	Method!
Reader 1:	But, what is a method?
Reader 2:	Instructions,
Reader 3:	directions, steps,
Reader 2:	a recipe for science.
Reader 1:	But why have a method?
Reader 3:	To guide the experiment,
Reader 2:	to find the answer to the purpose,
Reader 3:	to succeed.
Reader 1:	What happens if you don't follow the method?
Reader 2:	Could be dangerous!
Reader 3:	Experiments may not be successful.
Reader 1:	Okay, method is...
Reader 2:	a list of instructions to guide the person through the experiment.
Reader 1:	Example?
Reader 3:	Fill the jar one-half full with the soda.
Reader 2:	Add 1 teaspoon of salt to the soda.
Reader 1:	I got it!...Do you?
Reader 2:	Science!
Reader 3:	Experiments!
Reader 1:	Method!
All:	Fun!

Page 57: Science script: Method

Conclusions

Roles for Readers   **Student Names**

Reader 1   _____

Reader 2   _____

Reader 3   _____

Suggested Staging

Audience

Reader 1:	Science!
Reader 2:	Experiments!
Reader 3:	Conclusions!
Reader 1:	But, what are conclusions?
Reader 2:	The answers to your questions,
Reader 3:	the results of the experiment,
Reader 2:	that can confirm or disprove your hypothesis.
Reader 1:	What else can conclusions do?
Reader 3:	Stir up more questions,
Reader 2:	lead to new and different experiments,
Reader 3:	spark newfound interests in learning more about science.
Reader 1:	Okay, conclusions are...
Reader 2:	the results of this experiment with possible questions for further investigation.
Reader 1:	Example?
Reader 3:	When the salt is added to the cola, it pushes the bubbles of carbon dioxide out of the way.
Reader 2:	Replacing a gas with another substance is called effervescence.
Reader 1:	I got it!...Do you?
Reader 2:	Science!
Reader 3:	Experiments!
Reader 1:	Conclusions!
All:	Fun!

From: Building Connections: Learning with Readers Theatre by Dixon/Davies/Politano © 1995. May be reproduced for classroom use.

Page 57: Science script: Conclusions

Introducing the Library

Written and adapted for Readers Theatre by
Sue Postans and Cindy Lowry

Roles for Readers   **Student Names**

Reader 1   _____

Reader 2   _____

Librarian   _____

Suggested Staging

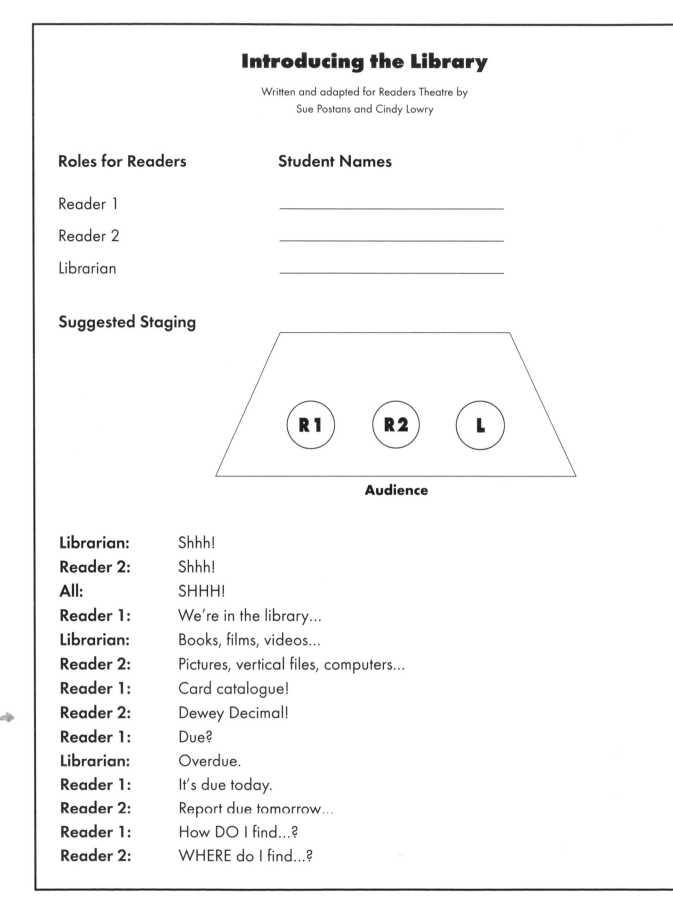

Audience

Librarian:	Shhh!
Reader 2:	Shhh!
All:	SHHH!
Reader 1:	We're in the library...
Librarian:	Books, films, videos...
Reader 2:	Pictures, vertical files, computers...
Reader 1:	Card catalogue!
Reader 2:	Dewey Decimal!
Reader 1:	Due?
Librarian:	Overdue.
Reader 1:	It's due today.
Reader 2:	Report due tomorrow...
Reader 1:	How DO I find...?
Reader 2:	WHERE do I find...?

Page 58: Library script, page 1

Reader 1:	Where's Waldo?
Librarian:	Magazines...
Reader 1:	National Geographic...
Reader 2:	Owl!
Librarian:	Sports Illustrated?
Reader 1:	Books!
Reader 2:	Fantasy, mystery, romance, fairy tales!
Reader 1:	Poetry, novels, stories!
Librarian:	FICTION!
Reader 2:	Biography, animals, space,
Reader 1:	dinosaurs, jokes, history,
Librarian:	nonfiction.
Reader 2:	It's raining outside.
Librarian:	Games, readings, story times!
Reader 1:	Time out!
Librarian:	It's sunny. Go outside.
Reader 1:	But Mrs. Library...
Librarian:	Outside!
Reader 1:	Awwww!
Reader 2:	School's closed!
Reader 1:	Oh no!
Reader 2:	Wait a minute.
Reader 1 & 2:	We can go to the public library!

Page 58: Library script, page 2

The Music Machine

Written and adapted for Readers Theatre by Sue Postans

Roles for Readers	Student Names
Narrator 1	_____
Narrator 2	_____
Jukebox	_____
Girl	_____
Boy	_____

(To begin, there could be strains of "The Music Goes Round and Round" played faintly.)

Narrator 1: Once upon a time there was an old jukebox sitting in the back corner of a cob-webby old garage. For many years it sat there silently, until one day a group of children playing nearby noticed that the door was open just a bit. Being well-brought-up children, they knew to respect private property and never go into a building uninvited, but somehow they knew it would be all right to go into this particular place. They carefully squeezed through the doorway and then saw the old jukebox.

Girl: What's that?

Boy: An old jukebox.

Girl: What's an old jukebox?

Boy: Oh, you know. It's a machine that plays music when you put in a quarter.

Girl: A music machine?

Narrator 2: They went closer, curious to see more.

Boy: Maybe if we plug it in, it will play for us.

Narrator 1: One of them found the plug.

Narrator 2: One of them found an electrical outlet.

Narrator 1: They plugged in the jukebox.

Narrator 1: and waited...

Narrator 2: and waited...

Narrator 1: nothing happened.

Girl: We have to turn it on, dude!

Narrator 2: They found a switch on the back of the juke box, and flipped it on.

Jukebox: Hi. I'm a magic music machine. I don't just play music; I can tell you what music is!

Boy: Sounds just like my music teacher.

Girl: Shhh!

Page 59: Music script, page 1

Boy:	What is music, Mr. Machine?
Jukebox:	Music is beat, melody, rhythm, texture, form and timbre.
Girl:	You're right, that sounds just like Mrs. Postans!
Jukebox:	Watch and listen!
Narrator 1:	The jukebox seemed to glow in the darkened garage. Suddenly a picture formed on its glass front.
Boy:	Just like a TV!
Girl:	Hey, isn't that a heart?
Jukebox:	You're right. The basis of all music is beat, and like your heart, it just keeps on going. It may be fast, like when you have run a race, or it may be slow, like when you wake up from a nap, but it keeps on going. What happens if your heart stops beating?
Boy:	You die.
Jukebox:	In other words, you stop, too, right? Well, when beat stops, so does the music. I think of the beat as walking.
Girl:	What else is in music?
Jukebox:	Rhythm!
Girl:	How do you spell that?
Boy:	R-H-Y-T-H-M.
Jukebox:	Right. Now rap it.
Girl:	R-H-Y...T-H-M! (*Can go on for a while. Then add*)
Boy:	BEAT-BEAT-BEAT-BEAT (*Do together a few times*)
Jukebox:	Rhythm is the long and short of your sound. You might say that the beat does the walking, but the rhythm does the talking.
Narrator 2:	A picture of feet and a mouth came up on the jukebox's screen.
Both:	(*Boy and Girl rap this together two or three times*) The beat does the walking and the rhythm does the talking. Ones the lips and the other on the stocking.
Girl:	Hey, that isn't all music is.
Jukebox:	No, as you walk along and talk, what are you hearing?
Girl:	I am hearing my voice.
Boy:	Yeah. When I'm going home from school, sometimes I hum a happy tune.
Girl:	Wait, isn't a hum part of music?
Jukebox:	Good for you. The hum is what we call melody, and it's the high and low of music, just as when you are talking, your voice goes higher and lower.
Boy:	It's like going up and down hills as you walk and talk.
Jukebox:	Wow, you have good ideas. Let me add that to my pictures of music. There, now we have pictures of feet, a mouth, some hills and valleys.
Girl:	Hey, this jukebox is a TV.
Jukebox:	Sort of. Now, when you walk by yourself, that's okay. What happens when a friend joins you?

Page 59: Music script, page 2

Boy:	We walk and talk and go up and down hills together?
Jukebox:	Yes. But does your friend walk the same or sound exactly the same as you?
Boy:	No.
Jukebox:	When several sounds get together, you hear what we call different timbres, or qualities, of sound. Here, let me add a picture of your friend.
Boy:	That doesn't look like my friend
Girl:	Shhh!
Jukebox:	Now sometimes, your friend may want to walk in a different rhythm, or sing in a different place, or even sing a different song from yours. But it can all still be a great sound, and we call that texture. It's like a layer cake of sound. Some layers are different from others, but together it's still a cake.
Girl:	Wow, I like your picture of a cake.
Jukebox:	One last part to the music. When that cake was baked, the baker couldn't just mix it in the air and throw it into the oven.
Boy:	My dad needs a bowl to mix the batter.
Girl:	My mom needs a cake pan to bake the cake in the oven.
Jukebox:	Well, the bowl or cake pan is like the last part of music we are going to talk about, which is called form. It is the container that gives it meaning or shape.
Boy:	I didn't realize music was like going for a walk!
Jukebox:	So now you know what is inside of me that allows you to hear music.
Girl:	Yeah, you have melody...
Boy:	and rhythm...
Girl:	timbre...
Boy:	texture...
Girl:	and form...
Boy:	The melody is the hum...
Girl:	as we walk to the beat...
Boy:	AND talk to the rhythm...
Girl:	We use different kinds of sounds to create timbre...
Boy:	and different layers to create texture...
Girl:	and put it all in some kind of form...
Both:	and we have MUSIC.
Girl:	I'll never go for another walk.
Boy:	Why?
Girl:	Too much happening. I'd get too tired to come home!
Jukebox:	Well, the magic is almost done for today. Please turn me off now, unplug me, and let me sleep. Come back another day and I will play for you again.
Narrator 1:	The children did as the jukebox asked. They crept out of the garage and carefully closed the door.

(Strains of "The Music Goes Round and Round" play as the children file offstage)

Page 59: Music script, page 3

Parent Night

Division _____

Roles for Readers	Student's name
Anchorperson 1 (AP1)	_____
Anchorperson 2 (AP2)	_____
On-site reporter 1 (R1)	_____
On-site reporter 2 (R2)	_____
On-site reporter 3 (R3)	_____
On-site reporter 4 (R4)	_____
On-site reporter 5 (R5)	_____
On-site reporter 6 (R6)	_____
On-site reporter 7 (R7)	_____
Interviewee 1 (I1)	_____
Interviewee 2 (I2)	_____
Interviewee 3 (I3)	_____
Interviewee 4 (I4)	_____
Interviewee 5 (I5)	_____
Interviewee 6 (I6)	_____
Interviewee 7 (I7)	_____
Advertiser 1 (A1)	_____
Advertiser 2 (A2)	_____
Advertiser 3 (A3)	_____
Advertiser 4 (A4)	_____
Advertiser 5 (A5)	_____
Advertiser 6 (A6)	_____
Advertiser 7 (A7)	_____
Advertiser 8 (A8)	_____

To stage the following piece, it is suggested that each pair of students be located around the perimeter of the room. Anchorperson 1 and 2 should be at the front as the focus of the audience returns to them after each report or commercial.

Page 82: Parent Night script, page 1

Anchorperson 1:	Good evening, listeners, I'm _____ [AP1].
Anchorperson 2:	And I'm _____ [AP2].
Anchorperson 1:	This is the evening news program from (*school initials and division number, e.g., MB12*).
Anchorperson 2:	brought to you live from _____ (*name of school and division number, e.g., Miracle Beach School, Division 12*)
Anchorperson 1:	Tonight we are going to introduce you to the program in which the _____ (*grade*) students will be involved this year. The teachers explained to us that all the different aspects of learning school are interwoven and connected. For these purposes, we're taking them apart to show you.
Anchorperson 2:	To help you understand this we have on-site reporters who will give us an in-depth focus on different aspects of life in the classroom. Now over to _____ [R1], who is one of our language arts reporters. Come in, _____ [R1].
Reporter 1:	Thank you, _____ [AP2] I have some interesting news about the writing section of the language arts program. One of the students is standing by to tell you about this. _____ [I1], what are the types of tasks you will be participating in this year?
Interviewee 1:	(*Description of the writing program inserted here*)
Reporter 1:	Thanks, _____ [I1]. As you can see, the students will be truly challenged with the writing tasks this year. This is _____ [R1] reporting from writing.
Anchorperson 1:	Thank you, _____ [R1]. Our other language arts reporter is _____ [R2]. What have you got for us, _____ [R2]?
Reporter 2:	Hi, _____ [AP1]. We have lots of information about reading. I have just been speaking to a number of students about the reading activities for this year, and here is _____ [I2] to summarize what they have told me.
Interviewee 2:	(*Description of reading program inserted here.*)
Reporter 2:	Great! Thanks, _____ [I2], that was most interesting, and of course best of luck for the year from all of us. That's all we have from here. _____ [R2] reporting.
Anchorperson 2:	Thank you, _____ [R2]. More news after this brief break.
Advertiser 1:	Say, what do you have for lunch at school each Friday?

Page 82: Parent Night script, page 2

Advertiser 2:	Hot dogs, of course!
Advertiser 1:	Really? How do you get them?
Advertiser 2:	Order them first thing on Friday morning, and pick them up at noon.
Advertiser 1:	Just hot dogs?
Advertiser 2:	No, you can get cookies, juice or milk as well.
Advertiser 1:	How much for all this?
Advertiser 2:	Hot dogs, _____, cookies, _____, and juice or milk, _____.
Advertiser 1:	That's great. I won't have to make my lunch on Thursday evenings! Every Friday you say?
Advertiser 2:	Yes, unless there is no school, and then it's the Thursday before.
Anchorperson 1:	Continuing with our story about Division _____ students, we go to _____ [R3].
Reporter 3:	Thanks, _____ [AP1]. Here I am surrounded by numbers in the math department where _____ [I3] is going to tell you about this year's program.
Interviewee 3:	(*Description of math program inserted here*)
Reporter 3:	It looks like a very interesting year for you in mathematics. Thanks, _____ [I3]. Now back to you, _____ [AP1] and _____ [AP2].
Anchorperson 2:	That's not my favourite subject, but each to his own. Now we have a report from _____ [R4] in science.
Reporter 4:	Right you are, _____ [AP2]. I have found my way through a maze of science equipment and come across _____ [I4] whose favorite subject is science. I'll let (her/him) tell you about the program.
Interviewee 4:	(*Description of science program inserted here*)
Reporter 4:	Fascinating topics for _____ (*grade*) students this year, _____ [AP1]. Now back to you.
Advertiser 3:	Noon hours are so boring. There's nothing to do.
Advertiser 4:	Hey, there's lots to do—just look around. There are kids playing soccer, throwing footballs, hitting softballs, skipping and playing on the adventure playground. What do you want to do?
Advertiser 3:	I guess any of those things. How do I sign up?

Page 82: Parent Night script, page 3

Advertiser 4:	You're new here, aren't you? You don't have to sign up. All you do is sign out equipment and get someone to play with.
Advertiser 3:	That's not too difficult. Would you like to play foursquare?
Advertiser 4:	Sure. Let's go and sign out a ball. I'll show you where.
Advertiser 3:	Noon hours don't have to be boring after all!
Anchorperson 2:	Standing by a map of Canada is our social studies reporter _____ [R5]. Come in, _____ [R5].
Reporter 5:	Yes, you're right, _____ [AP2]. I am standing by a map of Canada and a globe of the world. With me is _____, who has some facts about year _____ social studies. Hi, _____ [I5].
Interviewee 5:	Hi, _____ [R5]. (*Description of social studies program inserted here*)
Reporter 5:	So there you have it. Social studies in year _____. Now back to our hosts.
Anchorperson 1:	Well done, _____ [R5] and _____ [I5]. We have some more reporters out there. The next one is talking about my favourite thing. Are you there, _____ [R6]?
Reporter 6:	(*Puff*) Yes I am (*puff*), _____ [AP1]. I've just been playing a little one-on-one and (*puff*) am now trying to get my breath back. Not in as good shape as I thought. While I pause to catch my breath perhaps _____ [I6] can tell you about the various parts of the P.E. program.
Interviewee 6:	Sure can, and I can also beat _____ [R6] in one-on-one! (*Description of the P.E. program inserted here*)
Reporter 6:	Thanks, _____ [I6]. You not only gave me time to catch my breath, you also gave me a good explanation of the program. Now back to the studio after this break.
Advertiser 5:	I'm having difficulty with that kid there. He's trying to bully me into doing things I don't want to do.
Advertiser 6:	You could talk to a teacher or supervisor about it.
Advertiser 5:	I did, and they're looking out for me, but he doesn't come near me when they're around.
Advertiser 6:	The peacekeepers could help.
Advertiser 5:	How?

Page 82: Parent Night script, page 4

Advertiser 6:	They would allow you to discuss the problems with him while they listen in and assist you in talking it through. They would use Uncle Al's secret formula.
Advertiser 5:	Will they solve my problem?
Advertiser 6:	No, but they'll be able to provide some strategies that will help you deal with it.
Advertiser 5:	Well, I'll try them next time I need help.
Advertiser 6:	Good! I think you'll find them useful. Remember, they're the ones wearing red jackets.
Anchorperson 2:	I think we've covered most of our program for _____ (*division*), _____ (*year*). Of course if our listeners viewers have any questions, they can always phone _____ (*number*) and talk to the teacher or make an appointment.
Anchorperson 1:	That reminds me of reporting. You just spoke of reporting verbally. What other forms does reporting take for the students of _____?
Reporter 7:	Hello, _____ [AP1]. It's _____ [R7] here. Reporting is an area I have been covering and I have with me _____ [I7] who can provide an overview of the reporting process. Hello _____ [I7], please report.
Interviewee 7:	Sure thing, _____ [R7]. (*A description of process for reporting to parents inserted here.*)
Reporter 7:	I see the theme here as being one of keeping the communication lines open between home and school. I'm sure that will happen in _____. Now back to _____ [AP2] and _____ [AP1].
Anchorperson 2:	Thank you, _____ [R7]. Back for a wrap-up after this break.
Advertiser 7:	If I have to be absent from school for a day or more do I have to let the school know?
Advertiser 8:	Yes. Have your parent phone the school at _____ (*number*) before 9:00 a.m. so that we know you are safe at home.
Advertiser 7:	Do we have music classes at school?
Advertiser 8:	Yes, two periods a week with a music teacher in the music room. You can also be in the choir which meets noon hour on Wednesdays. Art and drama are also part of the program.

Page 82: Parent Night script, page 5

Advertiser 7: I guess these can be part of the rest of the day, too, you know, kind of integrated?

Advertiser 8: Yes...and you'll probably get some things to do at home, too. Teachers call that "homework"—you know, reading writing, studying math facts. Have a good year!

Anchorperson 1: Well, that's a brief overview of the program for _____ (grade) at _____ School.

Anchorperson 2: We hope that you now have a good idea of what to expect for your children this year.

Anchorperson 1: Remember, for more information or clarification you can always phone the school, at _____. Until next time, this is _____ [AP1] signing off...

Anchorperson 2: ...and _____ [AP2] saying goodnight, and we hope you all have a good year as part of _____ (grade) at _____ School.

Page 82: Parent Night script, page 6

Peacekeepers

written by Anne Davies in collaboration with
Heather Ferraby, Darry Oudendag and the Tsolum Peacekeepers.

Roles for Readers	Student Names
Reader 1 (R1)	_____
Reader 2 (R2)	_____
Reader 3 (R3)	_____
Reader 4 (R4)	_____
Reader 5 (R5)	_____
Reader 6 (R6)	_____
Reader 7 (R7)	_____
Reader 8 (R8)	_____
Reader 9 (R9)	_____
Reader 10 (R10)	_____
Reader 11 (R11)	_____
Reader 12 (R12)	_____
Reader 13 (R13)	_____
Reader 14 (R14)	_____
Reader 15 (R15)	_____
Reader 16 (R16)	_____
Reader 17 (R17)	_____
Reader 18 (R18)	_____
Reader 19 (R19)	_____
Reader 20 (R20)	_____
Reader 21 (R21)	_____
Reader 22 (R22)	_____
Fighter 1 (F1)	_____
Fighter 2 (F2)	_____
Fighter 3 (F3)	_____
Fighter 4 (F4)	_____
Fighter 5 (F5)	_____
Peacekeeper 1 (P1)	_____
Peacekeeper 2 (P2)	_____
Peacekeeper 3 (P3)	_____
Peacekeeper 4 (P4)	_____

Page 84: Peacekeeper script, page 1

Suggested Staging

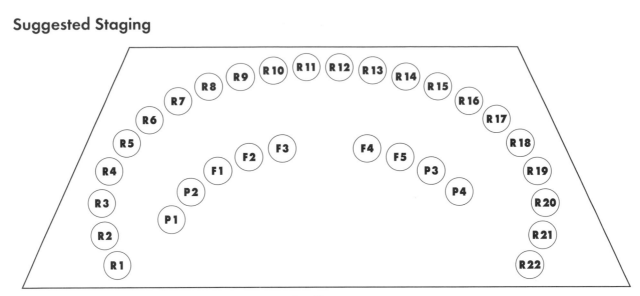

Audience

All readers face the audience. F1, F2, F3, F4, P1, P2, P3, P4 sit on floor with backs to the audience. Peacekeepers wear jackets and fighters wear hats.

Reader 14:	We listen.
Reader 15:	We are there.
Reader 17:	We like to chat.
Reader 19:	We are interested
Reader 20:	in what you have to say.
Reader 14:	We pay attention.
Reader 16:	We wear big,
Reader 17:	bright,
Reader 18:	red jackets,
Reader 19:	with a fish
Reader 20:	on a big T.
Reader 21:	We are trained to help you solve your problems.
Reader 22:	We won't walk away
Reader 21:	when you are talking to us.
Reader 23:	We won't walk away
Reader 21:	from a problem.

Page 84: Peacekeeper script, page 2

Reader 22:	Wc won't allow
Reader 21:	name calling,
Reader 23:	put-downs,
Reader 24:	or yelling.
Reader 21:	We won't walk away
Reader 22:	without your problem being solved.
Reader 1:	We are helpers,
Reader 3:	not police officers.
Reader 2:	A peacekeeper's job is to help
Reader 4:	students
Reader 5:	think of peaceful ways
Reader 6:	to solve their problems
Reader 4:	by themselves. We do *not* take sides.
Reader 5:	We listen to each of you.
Reader 8:	We try to be calm,
Reader 9:	patient,
Reader 7:	and friendly.
Reader 8:	We assist you
Reader 9:	to solve problems
Reader 10:	between yourselves and others.
Reader 11:	Some of the problems
Reader 12:	we help
Reader 13:	you solve are
Reader 11:	name-calling
Reader 12:	arguing,
Reader 13:	bullying,
Reader 12:	throwing things,
Reader 11:	using foul language,
Reader 13:	pushing,
Reader 11:	stealing,
Reader 12:	physical fights,

Page 84: Peacekeeper script, page 3

Reader 13:	spitting,
Reader 11:	disagreements in a game,
Reader 12:	teasing,
Reader 13:	blaming.
Reader 1:	We use
Reader 2:	Uncle Al's Formula.
Reader 2:	It is one way
Reader 3:	to find the best solution.
Reader 4:	Uncle Al's Formula
Reader 3:	has three parts.
Reader 5:	Step Number One:
Reader 6:	AGREE to solve the problem.
Reader 11:	*(Turn to R12 and use loud whisper)* Agree to solve the problem.
Reader 7:	Step Number Two:
Reader 8:	LISTEN to both sides.
Reader 12:	*(Turn to R13 and use loud whisper)* Listen to both sides.
Reader 9:	Step Number Three:
Reader 10:	SOLVE the problem.
Reader 13:	*(Turn to R11 and use loud whisper)* Solve the problem.

All readers bow their heads...they can look up after the fight starts.

F1, F2, P1, P2 count to three silently, saying to themselves: one-peacekeeper; two-peacekeeper; three-peacekeeper

They stand up; turn and face audience; start

Fighter 1:	Ow! Oh! Ah! Stop! That hurts!
Fighter 2:	Shut up! You're such a wimp.
Peacekeeper 1:	Sounds like there's a problem over there.
Peacekeeper 2:	Let's go check it out!
Peacekeeper 2:	Hi my name is _____ and this is _____.

Page 84: Peacekeeper script, page 4

Peacekeeper 3:	We are Peacekeepers. We're willing to help you solve your problem.
Peacekeeper 4:	We think you can work it out. Do you want to try?
Peacekeeper 3:	The ground rules for solving conflict are: tell the truth; don't interrupt; listen to each other;
Peacekeeper 3:	no name calling, blaming, or yelling.
Fighter 3:	I don't want to solve a stupid problem like this.
Fighter 4:	I want this to stop so this loser won't beat me up all the time.
Fighter 3:	Who are you calling a loser, you wimp!!??
Peacekeeper 4:	Excuse me, remember there's no name calling.
Peacekeeper 3:	Both of you will get a chance to tell what happened.
Peacekeeper 4:	You each have to listen while the other person is telling his/her side of the story. What happened?

All four peacekeeprs in red jackets step forward. Fighters step back.

All Peacekeepers:	After some talking, this problem was solved because the fighters wanted to solve it and the peacekeepers could help.

All peacekeepers kneel facing the audience.

Reader 14:	You can prevent peace by bringing fake problems,
Reader 17:	calling us names, fighting, swearing, disagreeing,
Reader 20:	fighting with each other and us, by following us around, or hitting us,
Reader 18:	by bugging us, pinching us, avoiding us, and hurting us.
Reader 21:	You can promote peace by
Reader 22:	being nice, saying hello,
Reader 21:	and bringing us your problems.
Reader 23:	By telling us your names,
Reader 1:	by using Uncle Al's Secret Formula,
Reader 12:	by agreeing to solve the problem.
Reader 23:	Letting us help
All:	YOU!
Reader 6:	We're here

Page 84: Peacekeeper script, page 5

Reader 7:	to help
All:	YOU!
Reader 9:	to solve your problems.
Reader 17:	We're here
Reader 18:	to help
Reader 19:	promote peace
Reader 20:	in the school.
Reader 14:	We're here to
All:	listen to your problems.
Reader 1:	We're here to make this
All:	a friendlier school.
Reader 5:	We're here to
All:	be friends.
Reader 16:	We're here to
All:	listen to you.

All stand and face audience; speak slowly with clear voices.

All Peacekeepers:	We're here to help you solve problems! We're here to make it safer AND MORE FUN on the playground!
All:	We're here to help you—WE ARE THE TSOLUM PEACEKEEPERS.

Tuck scripts under right arm. Silently count to three: one-peacekeeper, two-peacekeeper, three-peacekeeper. Raise heads and smile. Exit stage area by walking out to the right.

Page 84: Peacekeeper script, page 6

GLOSSARY

Articulation. A way of speaking or pronouncing.

Blocking. The position given to the readers on the stage.

Enunciation. Pronounciation of words and sentences clearly and distinctly.

Inflection. Modulation of voice, effected by change in tempo, tone, and pitch.

Offstage focus. Characters focus their eyes as if they were looking at the entire cast in a mirror located behind the audience. When their character is speaking to another character, the characters look at each other using the imaginary mirror image (see page 92).

Onstage focus. Characters address one another on the stage by looking directly at one another.

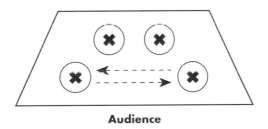

Audience

Projection. Ability to speak so voice can be heard by the entire audience.

Props (properties). Any movable articles used by performers to enhance their performances.

BIBLIOGRAPHY

Barchers, Suzanne I. *Readers Theater for Beginning Readers*. Englewood,
   Colorado: Teachers Ideas Press, 1993.

Barton, Bob. *Tell Me Another*. Markham, Ontario: Pembroke Publishing,
   1992.

Braun, W., and C. Braun. *Readers Theatre: Scripted Rhymes and Rhythms*.
   Calgary, AB: Braun and Braun Educational Enterprises Ltd., 1995.

———. *Readers Theatre: More Scripted Rhymes and Rhythms*. Calgary, AB:
   Braun and Braun Educational Enterprises Ltd., 1995.

British Columbia Ministry of Education. *Oral Communication in the
   Classroom*. Document XX0101. Victoria, B.C., January 1988.

Coger, Leslie Irene, and Melvin R. White. *Readers Theatre Handbook: A
   Dramatic Approach to Literature*. 3rd ed. Glenview, Illinois: Scott,
   Foresman, 1982.

Davies, Anne, Colleen Politano, Caren Cameron, and Kathleen
   Gregory. *Together Is Better*. Winnipeg: Peguis Publishers, 1992.

Davies, Anne, Colleen Politano, and Caren Cameron. *Making Themes
   Work*. Winnipeg: Peguis Publishers, 1993.

Fair, Sylvia. *The Bedspread*. New York: William Morrow, 1982.

Fredricks, Anthony D. *Frantic Frogs and Other Frankly Fractured Folk
   Tales for Readers Theater*. Englewood, Colorado: Teachers Ideas
   Press, 1993.

Hill, Susan. *Readers Theatre: Performing the Text*. Armadale, Australia:
   Eleanor Curtain Publishing, 1990.

Latrobe, Kathy Howard, and Mildred Knight Laughlin. *Readers Theatre
   for Young Adults*. Englewood, Colorado: Teachers Ideas Press, 1989.

———. *Readers Theatre for Children*. Englewood, Colorado: Teachers
   Ideas Press, 1989.

Long, Beverly Whitaker, and Mary Francis Hopkins. *Performing Literature*.
   Englewood Cliffs, N.J.: Prentice-Hall, 1982.

McTeague, Frank. *Shared Reading*. Markham, Ontario: Pembroke
   Publishing, 1992.

Northrop, Claire. *Around the World in Eighteen Plays: Folk-Tale Scripts for
   the Classroom*. Winnipeg: Peguis Publishers, 1994.

Politano, Colleen, and Anne Davies. *Multi-age and More*. Winnipeg:
   Peguis Publishers, 1994.

Rosen, Michael, and Helen Oxenbury. *We're Going On A Bear Hunt.* Walker Books: London, U.K., 1989.

Rylant, Cynthia. *When I Was Young In The Mountains.* New York: E.P. Dutton, 1982.

Scrivener, Louise M., and Dan Robinette. *A Guide to Oral Interpretation: Solo and Group Performance.* Indianapolis: Bobbs-Merrill Co., 1981.

Siamon, Sharon, and James Barry. *Skits and Scenes.* Scarborough, Ont.: Nelson, 1994.

Silverstein, Shel. "Ladies First." In *Free to Be You and Me.* Conceived by Marlo Thomas, developed and edited by Carole Hart, Letty Cottin Pogrebin, Mary Rodgers, Marlo Thomas. A Project of the Ms. Foundation, 39–45. McGraw Hill: New York, 1974

Sloyer, Shirlee. *Readers Theatre: Story Dramatization in the Classroom.* Urbana, Illinois: National Council of Teachers of English, 1982.

Thompson, Richard. *Cold Night, Brittle Light.* Victoria, B.C.: Orca Books, 1994.

Trelease, Jim, ed. *Read All About It!* New York: Penguin Books, 1993.

———. *Hey! Listen To This.* New York: Penguin Books, 1992.

———. *The New Read-Aloud Handbook.* New York: Penguin Books, 1989.

Prepared scripts are available from:

Take Part Productions Ltd.
Box 86756,
North Vancouver, B.C.
Canada V7L 4L3
phone/fax (604) 925-1989

Readers Theatre Script Service
P.O. Box 178333
San Diego, California
USA 92179
phone (619) 576-7369